Macarons

Macarons

50 exquisite recipes, shown in 200 beautiful photographs

Mowie Kay

aqua marine

This edition is published by Aquamarine,
an imprint of Anness Publishing Ltd,
Blaby Road, Wigston, Leicestershire LE18 4SE

info@anness.com

www.aquamarinebooks.com;
www.annesspublishing.com

If you like the images in this book and would like to investigate using them for publishing, promotions or advertising, please visit our website www.practicalpictures.com for more information.

© Anness Publishing Ltd 2013

A CIP catalogue record for this book is available from the British Library.

Publisher: **Joanna Lorenz**
Editor: **Kate Eddison**
Photographer and prop stylist: **Mowie Kay**
Food stylists: **Mowie Kay and Bruce Martin**
Designer: **Lisa Tai**
Production controller: **Mai-Ling Collyer**

PUBLISHER'S NOTE

Although the advice and information in this book are believed to be accurate and true at the time of going to press, neither the authors nor the publisher can accept any legal responsibility or liability for any errors or omissions that may have been made, nor for any inaccuracies nor for any loss, harm or injury that comes about from following instructions or advice in this book.

NOTES

- Bracketed terms are intended for American readers.
- For all recipes, quantities are given in both metric and imperial measures and, where appropriate, in standard cups and spoons. Follow one set of measures, but not a mixture, because they are not interchangeable.
- Standard spoon and cup measures are level. 1 tsp = 5ml, 1 tbsp = 15ml, 1 cup = 250ml/8fl oz.
- Australian standard tablespoons are 20ml. Australian readers should use 3 tsp in place of 1 tbsp for measuring small quantities.
- American pints are 16fl oz/2 cups. American readers should use 20fl oz/2.5 cups in place of 1 pint when measuring liquids.
- Electric oven temperatures in this book are for fan ovens. When using a conventional oven, the temperature will probably need to be increased by about 10–20°C/20–40°F. Since ovens vary, you should check with your manufacturer's instruction book for guidance.
- The nutritional analysis given for each recipe is calculated per portion (i.e. serving or item), unless otherwise stated. If the recipe gives a range, such as Serves 4–6, then the nutritional analysis will be for the smaller portion size, i.e. 6 servings. The analysis does not include optional ingredients, such as salt added to taste.
- Medium (US large) eggs are used unless otherwise stated.

Contents

Introduction

We have all gazed into the windows of patisseries, bakeries and cake shops, whether in France, Italy or anywhere else in the world, to see beautiful displays of delicate macarons in every colour imaginable. These elegant little morsels hide a secret simplicity behind their professional veneer, and this book reveals the tricks and techniques that will allow every home baker to create stunning macarons in their own kitchen.

The origins of the humble macaron are debatable and, contrary to popular belief, these delectable little desserts did not actually originate in France, but in Italy. The name 'macaron' is believed to be derived from the Italian word 'macaroni', which means fine dough. It is thought that macarons were brought to France by Catherine de Medici's pastry chefs in the 16th century. At this time, macarons were a single biscuit (cookie), and it was not until the early 20th century that two of the biscuits would be sandwiched together with a filling. This idea is most commonly accredited to the Parisian baker, Pierre Desfontaines, of the famous Ladurée bakery, where macarons were made popular by his creative use of ingredients and stunning presentation.

WHAT IS A MACARON?
A macaron is a small, fine, light and slightly chewy dessert made from two round almond cookies sandwiched together with a light filling. A distinct feature of a macaron is the 'foot': a small ruffling of the batter at the base of the macaron shells, caused as the shells rise in the oven during baking.

The classic French perfumed flavours, such as lavender, rose and violet, are used to create traditional macarons.

A macaron without these characteristic 'feet' is just not a macaron. A macaron can come in a variety of flavours and colours, and is never to be confused with a macaroon, the latter being a chunky coconut cookie. The classic macaron flavours, such as vanilla, strawberry, raspberry, chocolate or pistachio, are delicious. However, nowadays, the real fun of making (and tasting!) macarons is to experiment with new, different and exciting flavours, in a very similar way to the makers of the never-ending flavours of jelly beans that are available. The basic macaron shell is a simple mixture of ground almonds, icing (confectioners') sugar and egg whites, which all lend themselves very well to being a base for and absorbing most other flavours.

A variety of colours can be achieved by adding food colouring gel to the shells or fillings, or even both.

DIFFERENT TYPES OF MACARONS
The traditional macaron is small and round, and measures 4–5cm/1½–2in in diameter. This is the classic and much-loved macaron size and shape that has become popular all around the world. Slightly larger macarons are also fun to make and eat, and some people have even gone so far as to make

The range of colours and flavours is limited only by the baker's imagination.

Macarons are elegant, chic and beautiful, making them a popular choice for an afternoon tea selection.

large macaron cakes. For me, however, the main allures of macarons are their dainty size and the diversity of flavour combinations. I have therefore opted to keep all the macarons in this book the traditional 'mouthful' size, so you can savour a different flavour (and a different macaron) with each bite. The fillings of macarons were originally intended to be just a smear of something sticky and sweet, like a jam or jelly, to hold the two shells together. The filling options have now evolved into much more: buttercreams, spreads, pastes and whipped cream, for example. Since macaron shells are quite sweet just as they are, for this book I have tried to reduce the amount of sugar that goes into the fillings as much as possible. I like a simple whipped double (heavy) cream as my preferred base for a filling. This helps balance out the sweetness and allows the full flavour combinations to develop and unfurl on the palate.

MACARON SHAPES

Simple round shells are the classic shapes for macarons, and I have stuck to this throughout the book. However, it is very easy to form different shapes, if you want to add a new

element to your macarons: bunnies for Easter, hearts for Valentine's Day, snowmen for Christmas... Use your imagination, be creative, and you will find there is almost no limit to the different shapes you could come up with! A simple face can be piped on, or edible paint can be brushed on and topped with edible glitter. These basic decorating techniques can bring your shapes to life.

HOW TO USE THIS BOOK

Macarons may be challenging for new bakers. The quantities are tiny, the mixture is fairly unstable and the shells are delicate, so it can seem a daunting task. However, embarking on a macaron-making adventure is like the beginning of a life-long love affair, and you will not want to stop making them. Even better, once you get the knack for making them, it is like learning how to ride a bicycle – you never forget. Do not be limited by the flavours suggested in this book: you can mix and match the shells and fillings from different recipes, and come up with your own ideas as well. I have suggested variations throughout the book to give you extra inspiration, but I am sure you will think of many more!

Essential ingredients

You do not need much in your storecupboard and refrigerator to start making macarons. Just a few simple ingredients are required for the basic shells and fillings, and you will be whipping them up like a pastry chef in no time. However, a huge range of ingredients, flavourings and colourings can be used to create some very exciting combinations. It is vital to weigh or measure ingredients carefully, to ensure successful results.

The most important bit of advice I can give is to keep the ingredients for the shells as dry as possible. If you would like to add any ingredients that have some moisture in them, such as fruit, save these for the fillings. That way, you will ensure success.

Ground almonds
Made by grinding almonds together until fine and powdery, this is best bought ready-ground, to guarantee the lightness of the flour. When grinding nuts at home, too much grinding can lead to the flour becoming oily and heavy. Ground almonds is the ingredient that gives macarons their light and chewy texture, and it is also responsible for the characteristic macaron 'feet', which form at the base of the shells.

Sugar
Icing (confectioners') sugar is a main ingredient of macarons. This fine sugar is sifted with the ground almonds. It is

Fresh eggs.

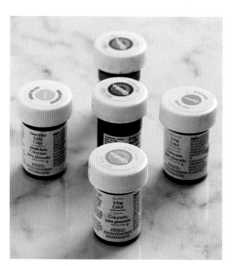

Food colouring gels.

this that gives the macarons their sweetness. Caster (superfine) sugar is also used in the shells, but this is added to the egg whites to form the meringue base.

Egg whites and egg white powder
Only the whites of eggs are needed to make macarons, and these are a key component to the texture and success of good macarons. Traditionally, egg whites need to be 'aged' before being used in macarons. This is done by by placing them in a bowl, covering in clear film (plastic wrap) and leaving them out to 'dry' for about 24 hours.

However, in this book, I use a mixture of egg whites and egg white powder. The egg white powder stabilizes the egg whites and reduces the need for 'aging'.

To avoid separating the yokes from the whites (saving time and money), you can now buy fresh egg whites in a packet. They are usually found in the

refrigerated aisles of supermarkets or health food stores. Egg white powder is usually found in the baking section of supermarkets. You will need both for my recipes. If, however, you choose to use fresh egg whites only, you should age them as described above.

Food colouring
In this book, I have used food colouring gel. Only a dab on the end of a cocktail stick (toothpick) is needed to obtain light pastel shades. Food colourings are also available in powdered form and these, although not as widely available, would also work well. Do not use liquid colouring in the shells, as the mixture should be as dry as possible.

Nuts
Any nuts, if ground into a fine powder, can be used to make a macaron base, either in place of ground almonds, or added to them. As a general rule, the oilier the nut, the more likely that it needs to be mixed with ground almonds.

Pistachio nuts.

The basic ingredients for macaron shells are shown clockwise (from top right): egg whites, caster sugar, egg white powder, ground almonds and icing sugar.

Fruits

Macaron shell ingredients absorb fruity flavours easily. When using citrus fruits, use only the grated rind in the shell mixture. This is to avoid adding liquid to the batter. Freeze-dried fruit is a great option, one that is becoming more widely available in supermarkets. If you cannot buy packets of them in your local supermarket, you can find it in some cereal mixes – since you only need a small amount, just pick some out of it! Fruit extracts can also be added to shells and fillings. Just 2–3 drops are needed – do not add too much to shell mixtures, as it will make the batter too moist. Avoid fruit essences, which have a synthetic taste and give inferior results than do extracts.

Unsweetened cocoa powder

Perfect for chocolate macarons, unsweetened cocoa powder is very rich, and only a little is needed each time. Already in powdered form, it is easily sifted with the other dry ingredients.

Coffee granules

All coffee-based macaron shells can be flavoured with instant coffee granules. These can be ground and sifted with the dry ingredients.

Cream

The fillings for the macarons in this book often contain lightly whipped double (heavy) cream. This provides moisture and acts as a light contrast to the sweet macaron shells.

Butter

To make smooth buttercreams, you need to have your butter at room temperature. Use unsalted butter.

Jams and jellies

Essential fillings, jams and jellies come in a wide variety of flavours and textures. Only a little is needed – just enough to hold the shells together.

Chocolate spreads and nut butters

Hazelnut and chocolate spread works well in many macarons, as does smooth peanut butter. Other sweet spreads and nut butters can also be used, if you have particular favourites.

Cream cheese

Ready to spread direct from the refrigerator, this adds a creaminess that works well with many flavours of sweet macaron shell.

Seeds

Topping macaron shells with seeds (or nuts) as soon as they are piped allows the topping to stick to the just-piped macaron batter. This adds texture, depth of flavour, and a pretty finish.

Spices

Often reserved for Christmas baking, spices provide tasty combinations in macarons. They are easy to use, as they can be bought in powdered form or can easily be ground or grated to a powder. Buy them in small quantities, as the flavours deteriorate quickly.

Cinnamon, nutmeg, cloves and star anise.

Essential equipment

Macarons are surprisingly easy to make, and you need only a few tools to bake like a pastry chef. There are lots of pricey tools, such as stand mixers, that will make short work of whipping up macaron mixtures, but they are not essential. Most people will be able to create professional-looking bites using equipment they already have tucked away in cupboards. If you do need to buy anything new, invest in the best quality you can afford.

The most important piece of equipment when making macarons is your oven. Spend some time getting to know how it works, and find out if it has an even distribution of heat. As a rule, modern fan ovens work much better than conventional ovens for baking macaron shells evenly, and for getting the perfect rise and foot formation. It is a good idea to invest in an oven thermometer to allow you to read the temperature of your oven accurately.

Kitchen scales
For macarons, it is essential that you weigh or measure all ingredients precisely. The ingredients are often in very tiny quantities, and it is vital to measure them accurately. I like to use a mixture of digital scales and measuring spoons. Your measuring spoon set must go down to at least ½ tsp, or ¼ tsp, if possible. Measuring cups are too inaccurate for very small quantities.

Mixing bowls and sieves.

Baking trays, baking parchment, piping bags and nozzles.

Baking tray
Nothing beats a good-quality, heavy baking tray. The most important aspect for macarons is that the tray is flat and straight, to keep the macarons' shapes and allow even distribution of heat. You may need to buy one, as most trays that come with ovens tend to be slanted to one side, to allow liquids and fats to drain away while cooking.

Baking parchment
The best baking parchment to use for making macarons is a non-stick greaseproof, waxed or silicone-lined variety. You can draw circles on to the paper, to use as a guide. Turn the paper over so that the ink is facing the tray, and use as a template to pipe perfect circles. Baking parchment works better than silicone mats, which tend to create distorted feet on the macarons.

Hand-held electric whisk, spatulas and balloon whisk.

A recent product on the market is a silicone macaron mat, which has small circular disc indentations set into the sheet for perfectly piped macarons every time. This should result in perfect circles, but, as with other silicone sheets, it interferes with the development of the macaron 'foot'.

Piping (pastry) bags and nozzles
The best piping bags to use for macarons are the plastic disposable bags. These are inexpensive and you avoid having to clean a reusable bag. You will need a plain round nozzle.

Electric food mixers
These are useful, but not essential, for making macarons. Mixers allow you to work hands-free, and to produce a fine meringue effortlessly for the first stage of the macaron mixture.

Electric hand whisk

Another very useful tool to have in any cook's kitchen, an electric whisk is a good investment for all bakers. It is much cheaper than an electric food mixer, but will make short work of beating egg whites and whipping cream. Although it is far more labour-intensive, a balloon whisk can often be used instead, if you do not have an electric whisk.

Spatula

An essential piece of equipment for combining the dry ingredients into the egg white mixture, a plastic or silicone spatula aids the folding process. When food colouring gel is added to the shell mixture, it is best scraped on to the tip of the spatula with a cocktail stick (toothpick), ensuring an even distribution of the food colouring gel while folding the wet and dry ingredients together.

Cocktail stick (toothpick)

These are useful for adding food colouring gel in small quantities. They are inexpensive and can be bought in most supermarkets.

Sieve (strainer)

This is one of the most important and least expensive pieces of equipment for making macarons. It is absolutely essential that each dry ingredient is sifted to ensure it is free of lumps, extremely fine and properly aerated. You will need a fine-meshed sieve to create the perfect mixture.

Cookie cutters

These can be used to create fun macaron shell shapes – perfect for parties or festive occasions. Place the cookie cutter on to the lined baking tray, and pipe the macaron batter into it. Only one cookie cutter is needed to make a whole tray of macarons, as you

Cocktail sticks are inexpensive and are handy for adding food colouring to batters.

can just lift it and move it along for the next one. Alternatively, you could lay a variety of cookie cutter shapes out on the baking tray. Try Easter bunnies, Christmas trees, stars or flowers.

PREPARING YOUR 'MISE EN PLACE'

The French term 'mise en place' means 'set in position', and it describes getting all the ingredients and equipment ready before you start baking. You will need two bowls: one for your dry ingredients, and one for your wet ingredients. You will also need a baking tray, piping (pastry) bag and plain round nozzle, sieve (strainer), a spatula, measuring spoons and all the ingredients listed in the macaron recipe you are going to bake. It is important to ensure that all your equipment is clean and grease-free, as the slightest trace of grease can prevent egg whites whisking perfectly. Having everything ready will mean there is less time for the macaron mixture to collapse.

1 *Line a large baking tray with a sheet of baking parchment. I find that one large baking tray is enough to hold 24 macaron shells (for making 12 macarons). However, if your trays are small, you should line two of them.*

2 *Fit your piping (pastry) bag with a plain round nozzle. Fold the tip in on itself and place the bag into a glass, so the tip is pointing upwards and no mixture will leak out. Fold the opening over the sides of the container, to hold the piping bag in place.*

Tips and techniques

The macaron recipes in this book have been designed to be as simple and fuss-free as possible. By just following the basic step-by-step method in each recipe, you can achieve great macarons easily. However, the macaron batter can be quite tricky to handle at times and can also be quite sensitive to temperature, humidity and other environmental factors, as well to as the quality and freshness of ingredients.

The following advice will help the novice home baker achieve professional-looking results with every batch of macarons. Here, I will guide you step by step through every stage of making the shells, from weighing out ingredients to piping perfect circles. It is worth reading through this section before you embark on making your first batch of macarons. You should have got your 'mise en place' ready at this stage (*see page 11*): your equipment clean and dry, your baking tray lined, your piping (pastry) bag prepared, and your ingredients at room temperature.

SIFTING, SIFTING, SIFTING
I cannot stress enough how important it is to sift all your dry ingredients. This includes powders, flours, granules, and any other dry ingredient that can fit through a sieve (strainer). If possible, sift each dry ingredient two or three times, to ensure that it is aerated and very fine. A typical macaron batter can handle only around 10g/¼oz of unsifted ingredients; any more than this, and the macaron shells can look chunky and uneven.

MEASURING OUT THE INGREDIENTS
This is where digital scales come into their own, as some of the ingredients are measured out in tiny quantities.

1 *Weigh out your liquid egg whites, and place them in a grease-free mixing bowl. Use a stainless-steel bowl, if you prefer, which can help to stabilize the egg whites.*

2 *Weigh out the caster (superfine) sugar, then sift it into the egg whites. This allows the sugar to start dissolving. Weigh out the egg white powder, and sift it in. Set aside.*

3 *Weigh out the ground almonds and icing (confectioners') sugar, and sift them into a separate, grease-free bowl. Weigh and sift in any other dry ingredients needed.*

MAKING MACARON MIXTURE

At this stage, you should have a bowl of dry ingredients: ground almonds, icing (confectioners') sugar, and any other dry flavourings. Another bowl contains a wet mixture: liquid egg whites, caster (superfine) sugar and egg white powder. These two mixtures now need to be brought together in a specific way. The method of mixing the two together is vital, if you want to create perfect macaron shells. For this stage, you should have your whisk and spatula ready, as well as a cocktail stick (toothpick) and food colouring gel, if you plan to add any colour to your macaron shells.

1 *Whisk the egg whites with the caster (superfine) sugar and egg white powder, until stiff peaks form. Stiff peaks are achieved when the whisk is slowly lifted out of the meringue, and the egg whites leave peaks that remain upright. If the peaks fold downwards (in soft peaks), the meringue is not ready. Care must be taken not to over-whisk the meringue at this stage, as it can result in dry macarons. If the meringue becomes chunky and clumps together, it has been over-whisked. If this happens, unfortunately, it is difficult to resurrect the mixture, so it is best to start again.*

2 *Using a spatula, transfer the meringue mixture to the bowl containing the sifted ground almonds and icing (confectioners') sugar, and any other ingredients needed for that recipe.*

3 *Any food colouring should be added now. Start by gently scraping half a circle around the inside of the bowl, and ending by folding this into the middle of the bowl. Turn the bowl and repeat. This folding process is important. It may not look like it is mixing well at the start, but this changes quickly at the end, and it is important not to over-fold. (Under-folding results in quite a thick batter that does not move, and over-folding results in a batter that is too runny.)*

4 *To check that you have achieved the perfect consistency, lift some of the mixture up, and tilt the spatula to allow the mixture to fall back into the bowl. It should fall from the spatula in long, smooth 'ribbons' that fall slowly. The ribbons should retain their shape for 20–30 seconds once they have fallen back in the bowl. If the ribbons lose their shape too quickly, the batter has been over-mixed. If the ribbons do not lose their shape at all, the batter is under-mixed and will need a few more folds. Personally, I have found that the ideal number of folds is 60–80. Counting folds might seem unnecessary, but it is helpful for beginners who are just getting to grips with how the mixture should look and feel.*

ADDING COLOUR

Food colouring gels and pastes come in such a large variety of shades, the options for macarons are endless. Also, you can mix two or more colours to achieve the perfect shade. Before you begin folding the mixture, dip a cocktail stick (toothpick) in the food colouring gel, and scrape this on to your spatula. Now, as you fold, the colour will be evenly distributed.

PIPING AND DRYING MACARONS

Your macaron mixture is now ready for piping. Work quickly, while the mixture is the correct consistency.

1 *Transfer the mixture to the prepared piping (pastry) bag, which should be in a glass or other cylindrical container (see page 11), making it easy to fill. Remove the filled piping bag from its container and slowly start squeezing the mixture down to the tip of the bag. Using two hands, hold your piping bag above your lined baking tray. Hovering just a few millimetres, or a fraction of an inch, from the baking tray, squeeze a small amount of batter on to the tray, until it forms a 4cm/1½in circle (or enough to fill the circle on your template, if you have made one), then lift the bag upwards and stop squeezing.*

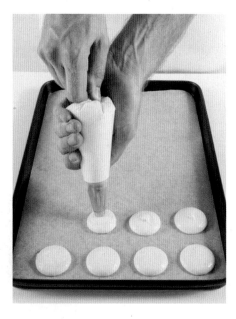

2 *Repeat for the whole tray (the mixtures in this book make 24 shells). Any peaks on the shells should soon disappear, leaving smooth circles. If, by the time you have piped a row of macarons, the first shells still have peaks, it means the batter is still too thick. In this case, simply scrape the batter off the tray with a spatula, place all the batter back into the bowl, and fold it a few more times. Once you have piped all your shells, preheat the oven to 130°C/250°F/Gas ½.*

3 *At this point, you can decorate the macarons with nuts, dried fruits, ground spices, or other flavourings. Sprinkle over or arrange the decorations on half of the shells (these will be the tops of the finished macarons) and leave the rest of the macaron shells plain (these will be the bottoms).*

4 *If you are short of time, you can place the tray in your preheated oven immediately – the macarons will still turn out well. However, if you allow some drying time, the texture of the shell is better, creating the typical combination of a crispy outside and a chewy inside. Simply leave the tray out in a warm, dry room for a minimum of 15 minutes, or for as long as 1 hour, until the piped shells have formed a 'skin' and do not yield when touched very lightly with a finger.*

DRYING TIPS

I find a good spot for drying the macarons is in the kitchen above the preheating oven. Humidity can adversely affect the shape and texture of the shells, so it is advised not to start washing up until the macarons shells are safely in the oven.

BAKING MACARONS

After 15 minutes of drying, your macaron shells are now ready to be baked.

1 *Place the macarons in the preheated oven, and bake for about 10 minutes. The first time you bake macarons, it is advisable to set your alarm for 5 minutes, and check them periodically from that moment, as all ovens vary. Do not let the macaron shells brown at all, as that will affect their delicate colour. The shells should have risen, be firm when touched gently with a finger, and have characteristic 'feet' at the base.*

2 *Remove the macarons from the oven as soon as they are cooked, but not browned at all. Leave them on the baking tray until cool. They may be stuck to the baking parchment at first, but they usually lift off easily once they have cooled to room temperature. Do not try to remove them too soon, or they may break.*

3 *Once they are completely cool, and can be moved around freely on the baking parchment, you can transfer the shells to a cooling rack. Handle the cooked shells carefully, as they are very delicate. I have squashed many a macaron shell by being heavy-handed with them!*

BAKING TIMES AND TEMPERATURES

Knowing your oven is one of the key factors in successful macarons. Oven temperatures vary from one model to the next, and from the top of the oven to the bottom, as well as from left to right. I have always said that one of the best ways to detect your oven's faults is to bake a batch of macarons in it. Macaron shells are delicate in nature and are subject to even the slightest changes in temperature. Thus, if the oven is a little hotter on the right side, the macarons to the right of the baking tray rise first and get 'feet' first, followed by those to the left. Meanwhile, the ones to the right start to brown, so, if this is the case, it is best to turn the tray around halfway through baking to allow for even cooking.

Some ovens only heat from above, so it is then advisable to place the baking tray below the middle of the oven. A little experimentation is necessary and there is nothing better with which to experiment than macarons. Macarons do not need long baking times; usually about 10 minutes should suffice, any longer and they could start to discolour or turn brown, which ruins the pretty pastel shades. Again, this all depends on your oven. All temperatures given in this book are for fan ovens, as these tend to be the most consistent for making successful macarons. If using a conventional oven, increase the recommended temperatures by 20°C/40°F. However, this all depends on your oven and should just be used for guidance.

STORAGE

The flavour and texture of macaron shells usually develop and improve after 1–2 days. The best ways of storing macarons is in an airtight container in the refrigerator for up to 1 week. This applies to unfilled shells only. It is best to add the fillings on the day you are serving them; if you fill them in advance, the macaron shells become soggy.

Macaron shells can be made in advance.

You can freeze the unfilled macaron shells for up to 1 month. This actually improves the taste and texture of macarons, making them chewier. Defrost the shells before filling them. Once filled, it is best to eat macarons immediately, and definitely on the same day of filling.

Macarons topped with candied fruit.

Macarons topped with ground nuts.

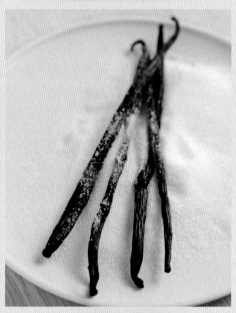

Classics

Traditional French flavours are found in the
pages of this first chapter, from the lovely
vanilla macaron to the moreish pistachio
macaron and the decadent chocolate macaron.
Their simplicity is what makes them classic,
and these will be tastiest when made with
top-quality ingredients – use vanilla seeds
instead of vanilla extract, and good-quality
chocolate, to achieve the best flavours.

Vanilla macarons

Create the classic vanilla macaron by using vanilla seeds scraped from a pod to guarantee that the best flavour is achieved. In my opinion, it is pleasing to see the little specks of vanilla seeds in any home-baked product. You can buy vanilla sugar, or make your own by placing a scraped pod in a jar of caster sugar.

Makes | 12 macarons

For the shells
60g/2¼oz egg whites
60g/2¼oz/generous ¼ cup caster (superfine) sugar
7.5ml/1½ tsp egg white powder
120g/4¼oz/generous 1 cup icing (confectioners') sugar
60g/2¼oz/generous ½ cup ground almonds
seeds of 1 vanilla pod (bean)
vanilla sugar, for sprinkling

For the filling
80g/3¾oz/scant ¾ cup icing (confectioners') sugar
40g/1½oz/3 tbsp unsalted butter, softened
20ml/4 tsp double (heavy) cream
seeds of 1 vanilla pod (bean)

VARIATION
Fill with a tiny scoop of ice cream.

1 Line a baking tray with non-stick baking parchment. Fit a piping (pastry) bag with a plain round tip.

2 Place the egg whites in a clean bowl, and sift the caster sugar and egg white powder over the egg whites. Whisk with an electric mixer until stiff peaks form.

3 In a separate bowl, sift together the icing sugar and ground almonds. Add the vanilla seeds and the egg white mixture to the almond mixture. Using a spatula, gently fold the mixture until it falls in ribbons when lifted with the spatula.

4 Fill the piping bag with the mixture, and pipe 24 4cm/1½in rounds on to the lined baking tray. Sprinkle with vanilla sugar. Preheat the oven to 130°C/250°F/ Gas ½, and leave the baking tray out in a warm, dry room for at least 15 minutes.

5 Place the tray in the middle of the oven and bake for 10 minutes. Remove from the oven and allow to cool.

6 To make the filling, place the icing sugar and butter in a bowl, and whisk until crumbly. Add the double cream and vanilla seeds, and whisk until you have a smooth vanilla buttercream.

7 To fill the macarons, place a teaspoonful of buttercream on to the flat side of one macaron shell and top with the flat side of another. Repeat to make 12 macarons.

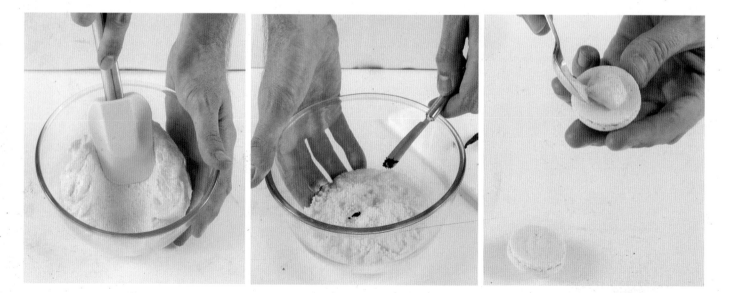

Per Macaron: Energy 153kcal/644kJ; Protein 2g; Carbohydrate 23.2g, of which sugars 22.9g; Fat 6.4g, of which saturates 2.5g; Cholesterol 9mg; Calcium 17mg; Fibre 0g; Sodium 43mg

Chocolate macarons

A rich and luxurious macaron, this is by far the easiest macaron recipe to make. Crisp macaron shells are flavoured with cocoa powder, and filled with a luxurious chocolate ganache. I like to decorate half of them with a sprinkle of cocoa powder on top, for a bit of variation.

Makes | 12 macarons

For the shells
60g/2¼oz egg whites
60g/2¼oz/generous ¼ cup caster (superfine) sugar
7.5ml/1½ tsp egg white powder
120g/4¼oz/generous 1 cup icing (confectioners') sugar
50g/2oz/½ cup ground almonds
8g/¼oz unsweetened cocoa powder

For the filling
75g/3oz dark (bittersweet) chocolate
60ml/4 tbsp single (light) cream

For decorating
unsweetened cocoa powder, for sprinkling (optional)

COOK'S TIP
Use a good-quality dark chocolate with over 70 % cocoa solids for the best flavour.

1 Line a baking tray with non-stick baking parchment. Fit a piping (pastry) bag with a plain round tip.

2 Place the egg whites in a clean bowl, and sift the caster sugar and egg white powder over the egg whites. Whisk with an electric whisk until stiff peaks form.

3 In a separate bowl, sift together the icing sugar, ground almonds and cocoa. Add the egg white mixture to the almond mixture. Using a spatula, gently fold the mixture until the batter falls in ribbons when lifted with the spatula.

4 Fill the piping bag with the mixture and pipe 24 4cm/1½in rounds on to the lined baking tray. Preheat the oven to 130°C/250°F/Gas ½, and leave the baking tray out in a warm, dry room for at least 15 minutes.

5 Place the tray in the middle of the oven and bake for 10 minutes. Remove from the oven and allow to cool.

6 For the chocolate ganache filling, place the chocolate and cream in a non-stick pan, and heat over a low heat, stirring, until melted and well combined. Remove from the heat and allow to cool, stirring occasionally, until thickened.

7 To fill the macarons, place a teaspoonful of chocolate ganache on to the flat side of one macaron shell, and top with the flat side of another. Repeat to make 12 macarons. Sprinkle the tops of some of the macarons with cocoa powder, if you like.

Per Macaron: Energy 91kcal/393kJ; Protein 2.4g; Carbohydrate 9.7g, of which sugars 9.4g; Fat 5.1g, of which saturates 1.8g; Cholesterol 2.7mg; Calcium 18mg; Fibre 0.6g; Sodium 30mg

Pistachio macarons

A firm favourite among my friends, and one of the classic French flavours, these pistachio macaron shells are filled with a sumptuous dark chocolate ganache. Chocolate buttercream also works well as a filling. If you are feeling adventurous, try pineapple jam – the combination with pistachio is unusual and exciting.

Makes | 12 macarons

For the shells
60g/2¼oz egg whites
60g/2¼oz/generous ¼ cup caster
  (superfine) sugar
7.5ml/1½ tsp egg white powder
120g/4¼oz/generous 1 cup icing
  (confectioners') sugar
60g/2¼oz/generous ½ cup
  ground pistachios
extra pistachios, roughly chopped,
  for sprinkling

For the filling
60ml/4 tbsp single (light) cream
75g/3oz dark (bittersweet) chocolate

COOK'S **TIP**
You can buy ground pistachios from large supermarkets, but grinding your own will guarantee the freshest flavour. Use a clean spice or coffee grinder.

1 Line a baking tray with non-stick baking parchment. Fit a piping (pastry) bag with a plain round tip.

2 Place the egg whites in a clean bowl, and sift the caster sugar and egg white powder over the egg whites. Whisk with an electric mixer until stiff peaks form.

3 In a separate bowl, sift together the icing sugar and ground pistachios. Add the egg white mixture to the dry mixture. Gently fold together until the batter falls in ribbons when lifted with the spatula.

4 Fill the piping bag with the mixture and pipe 24 4cm/1½in rounds on to the lined baking tray. Sprinkle half the shells with chopped pistachios (these will be the tops). Preheat the oven to 130°C/250°F/Gas ½. Leave the baking tray out in a warm, dry room for 15 minutes.

5 Place the tray in the middle of the oven and bake for 10 minutes. Remove from the oven and allow to cool.

6 For the filling, heat the cream in a non-stick pan until it just starts to bubble. Place the dark chocolate in a heatproof bowl, and pour the cream over. Whisk together until the chocolate has melted. Allow to cool, stirring occasionally, until thickened.

7 To fill the macarons, place a teaspoonful of chocolate ganache on to the flat side of an undecorated macaron shell, and top with the flat side of a decorated macaron shell. Repeat to make 12 macarons.

Per Macaron: Energy 149kcal/626kJ; Protein 2.8g; Carbohydrate 20.5g, of which sugars 20.1g; Fat 6.8g, of which saturates 2g; Cholesterol 3mg; Calcium 22mg; Fibre 0.4g; Sodium 36mg

Lemon macarons

Zesty undertones in the shell combine with a creamy lemon filling to give these macarons a citrus kick that is perfectly balanced between tart and sweet. Do not overdo the food colouring in the shells – these macarons look prettiest when they are a pastel shade of yellow.

Makes | 12 macarons

For the shells
60g/2¼oz egg whites
60g/2¼oz/generous ¼ cup caster (superfine) sugar
7.5ml/1½ tsp egg white powder
120g/4¼oz/generous 1 cup icing (confectioners') sugar
60g/2¼oz/generous ½ cup ground almonds
finely grated rind of 1 lemon
yellow food colouring gel

For the filling
80g/3¾oz/scant ¾ cup icing (confectioners') sugar
40g/1½oz/3 tbsp unsalted butter, softened
20ml/4 tsp double (heavy) cream
3–4 drops of lemon extract
yellow food colouring gel

VARIATION
Use store-bought lemon curd instead of the lemon buttercream.

---

1 Line a baking tray with non-stick baking parchment. Fit a piping (pastry) bag with a plain round tip.

2 Place the egg whites in a clean bowl, and sift the caster sugar and egg white powder over the egg whites. Whisk with an electric mixer until stiff peaks form.

3 In a separate bowl, sift together the icing sugar, ground almonds and lemon zest. Add the egg white mixture to the almond mixture. Dip a cocktail stick (toothpick) into the food colouring gel, and scrape this on to the tip of a spatula. Use the spatula to fold the mixture gently until the batter falls in ribbons when lifted with the spatula.

4 Fill the piping bag with the mixture. Pipe 24 4cm/1½in rounds on to the baking tray. Preheat the oven to 130°C/250°F/Gas ½. Leave the baking tray out in a warm, dry room for 15 minutes.

5 Place the tray in the middle of the oven and bake for 10 minutes. Remove from the oven and allow to cool.

6 To make the lemon buttercream filling, place the icing sugar and butter in a bowl, and whisk until crumbly. Add the double cream and lemon extract, and whisk until smooth. Dip a cocktail stick into the food colouring gel and scrape this into the buttercream mixture. Whisk well, until evenly yellow.

7 To fill the macarons, place a teaspoonful of lemon buttercream on to the flat side of one macaron shell and top with the flat side of another. Repeat to make 12 macarons.

Energy 153kcal/644kJ; Protein 2g; Carbohydrate 23.2g, of which sugars 22.9g; Fat 6.4g, of which saturates 2.5g; Cholesterol 9mg; Calcium 17mg; Fibre 0g; Sodium 43mg

Violet macarons

These macarons are one of the classic flavours, and they capture the taste of French pastry at its finest. Using violet sugar instead of caster (superfine) sugar turns the colour of the macarons a deep violet, without needing to add food colouring. The sugar gives a subtle flavour that is not overpowering.

Makes | 12 macarons

For the shells
60g/2¼oz egg whites
60g/2¼oz/generous ¼ cup
  violet sugar
7.5ml/1½ tsp egg white powder
120g/4¼oz/generous 1 cup icing
  (confectioners') sugar
60g/2¼oz/generous ½ cup
  ground almonds

For the filling
80g/3¾oz/scant ¾ cup icing
  (confectioners') sugar
40g/1½oz/3 tbsp unsalted
  butter, softened
20ml/4 tsp double (heavy) cream
purple food colouring gel

COOK'S **TIP**
Violet sugar adds a stunning colour and taste. It is available from specialist baking stores.

1 Line a baking tray with non-stick baking parchment. Fit a piping (pastry) bag with a plain round tip.

2 Place the egg whites in a clean bowl, and sift the violet sugar and egg white powder over the egg whites. Whisk with an electric mixer until stiff peaks form.

3 In a separate bowl, sift together the icing sugar and ground almonds. Add the egg white mixture to the almond mixture. Using a spatula, gently fold the mixture until the batter falls in ribbons when lifted with the spatula.

4 Fill the piping bag with the mixture and pipe 24 4cm/1½in rounds on to the lined baking tray. Preheat the oven to 130°C/250°F/Gas ½, and leave the baking tray out in a warm, dry room for at least 15 minutes.

5 Place the tray in the middle of the oven and bake for 10 minutes. Remove from the oven and allow to cool.

6 To make the filling, place the icing sugar and butter in a bowl, and whisk until crumbly. Add the double cream and whisk until smooth. Dip a cocktail stick (toothpick) into the food colouring gel, and scrape this into the buttercream mixture. Whisk well, until evenly coloured.

7 To fill the macarons, place a teaspoonful of buttercream on to the flat side of one macaron shell and top with the flat side of another. Repeat to make 12 macarons.

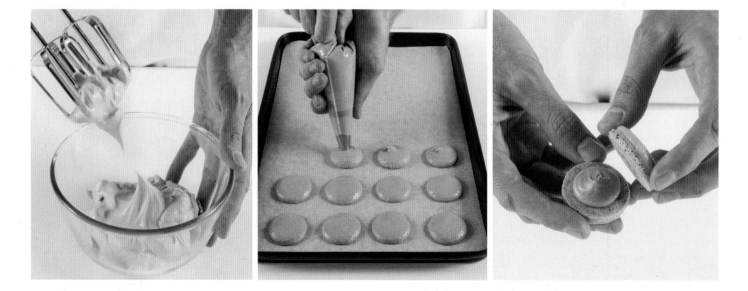

Per Macaron: Energy 153kcal/643kJ; Protein 2.1g; Carbohydrate 23.1g, of which sugars 22.9g; Fat 6.4g, of which saturates 2.5g; Cholesterol 9mg; Calcium 17mg; Fibre 0g; Sodium 42mg

Rose macarons

These macarons are a floral bouquet for the palate. A delightful and fresh-tasting treat, with rose extract in the the shells and buttercream. These can also be filled with plain whipped cream.

Makes | 12 macarons

For the shells
60g/2¼oz egg whites
60g/2¼oz/generous ¼ cup caster (superfine) sugar
7.5ml/1½ tsp egg white powder
120g/4¼oz/generous 1 cup icing (confectioners') sugar
60g/2¼oz/generous ½ cup ground almonds
2–3 drops of rose extract
red food colouring gel

For the filling
80g/3¾oz/scant ¾ cup icing (confectioners') sugar
40g/1½oz/3 tbsp unsalted butter, softened
20ml/4 tsp double (heavy) cream
2–3 drops of rose extract
red food colouring gel

1 Line a baking tray with non-stick baking parchment. Fit a piping (pastry) bag with a plain round tip.

2 Place the egg whites in a clean bowl, and sift the caster sugar and egg white powder over the egg whites. Whisk with an electric mixer until stiff peaks form.

3 In a separate bowl, sift together the icing sugar and ground almonds. Add the egg white mixture to the almond mixture. Add the rose extract. Dip a cocktail stick (toothpick) into the food colouring gel, and scrape this on to the tip of a spatula. Use the spatula to fold the mixture gently, until the colour is even and the batter falls in ribbons when lifted with the spatula.

4 Fill the piping bag with the mixture and pipe 24 4cm/1½in rounds on to the lined baking tray. Preheat the oven to 130°C/250°F/Gas ½. Leave the baking tray out in a warm, dry room for at least 15 minutes.

5 Place the tray in the middle of the oven and bake for 10 minutes. Remove from the oven and allow to cool.

6 For the filling, place the icing sugar and butter in a bowl. Whisk until crumbly. Add the double cream and rose extract, and whisk until smooth. Dip a cocktail stick into the food colouring gel, and scrape it into the buttercream. Whisk well, until evenly coloured.

7 To fill the macarons, pipe the filling on to the flat side of one macaron shell and top with the flat side of another. Repeat to make 12 macarons.

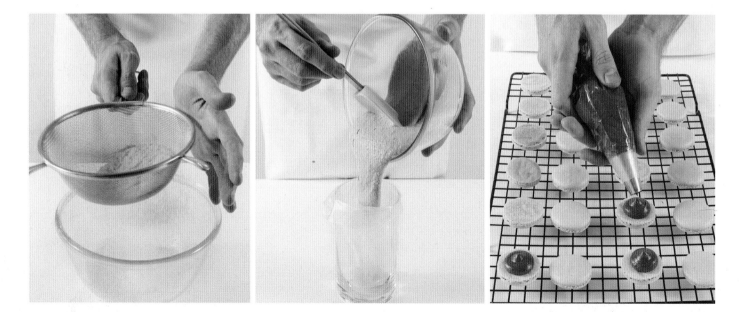

Per Macaron: Energy 153kcal/643kJ; Protein 2g; Carbohydrate 23.2g, of which sugars 22.8g; Fat 6.4g, of which saturates 2.5g; Cholesterol 9mg; Calcium 15mg; Fibre 0g; Sodium 43mg

Lavender macarons

In southern France, lavender has been used to impart a perfumed taste in cooking and baking for many years. Make your own lavender sugar by placing edible lavender flowers in a bowl of sugar for 1 week.

Makes | 12 macarons

For the shells
60g/2¼oz egg whites
60g/2¼oz/generous ¼ cup caster (superfine) sugar
7.5ml/1½ tsp egg white powder
120g/4¼oz/generous 1 cup icing (confectioners') sugar
60g/2¼oz/generous ½ cup ground almonds
violet food colouring gel
edible dried lavender flowers or petals, for sprinkling

For the filling
100ml/3½fl oz/scant ½ cup double (heavy) cream
15ml/1 tbsp lavender sugar
edible dried lavender flowers or petals, for sprinkling

1 Line a baking tray with non-stick baking parchment. Fit a piping (pastry) bag with a plain round tip.

2 Place the egg whites in a clean bowl, and sift the caster sugar and egg white powder over the egg whites. Whisk with an electric mixer until stiff peaks form.

3 In a separate bowl, sift together the icing sugar and ground almonds. Add the egg white mixture to the almond mixture. Dip a cocktail stick (toothpick) into the food colouring gel, and scrape this on to the tip of a spatula. Use the spatula to fold the mixture gently, until the colour is even and the batter falls in ribbons when lifted with the spatula.

4 Fill the piping bag with the mixture. Pipe 24 4cm/1½in rounds on to the baking tray. Sprinkle half the shells with lavender flowers (these will be the tops). Preheat the oven to 130°C/250°F/Gas ½, and leave the baking tray out in a warm, dry room for at least 15 minutes.

5 Place the tray in the middle of the oven and bake for 10 minutes. Remove from the oven and allow to cool.

6 For the filling, whip the cream with the sugar until thick. Place a teaspoonful of lavender cream on to the flat side of an undecorated macaron shell, sprinkle with lavender flowers, and top with the flat side of a decorated macaron shell. Repeat to make 12 macarons.

Per Macaron: Energy 140kcal/586kJ; Protein 2.1g; Carbohydrate 17.6g, of which sugars 17.3g; Fat 7.3g, of which saturates 3g; Cholesterol 11mg; Calcium 18mg; Fibre 0g; Sodium 23mg

Caramel, Chocolate and Coffee

An indulgent collection of macarons awaits
you in this chapter. It is packed with rich and
luxurious ingredients, such as dulce de leche,
Vietnamese coffee and chocolate spread.
This section also explores a few classic flavour
combinations that are popular worldwide,
such as chocolate and cherry, salted caramel,
mocha, and banoffee.

Salted caramel macarons

Sweet and salty has always been a very enticing flavour combination, and it has never been better than here in these delectable macarons. Sprinkle more salt on to the tops of the macarons for a little crunch and extra saltiness – I tend to use low-sodium salt flakes for these.

Makes | 12 macarons

For the shells
60g/2¼oz egg whites
60g/2¼oz/generous ¼ cup caster (superfine) sugar
7.5ml/1½ tsp egg white powder
120g/4¼oz/generous 1 cup icing (confectioners') sugar
60g/2¼oz/generous ½ cup ground almonds
orange food colouring gel
low-sodium salt flakes, for sprinkling

For the filling
100ml/3¾fl oz/scant ½ cup dulce de leche

> **COOK'S TIP**
> Dulce de leche is made by gently heating sweetened condensed milk until caramelized. It is not easy to make at home, but it can be bought in most supermarkets.

1 Line a baking tray with non-stick baking parchment. Fit a piping (pastry) bag with a plain round tip.

2 Place the egg whites in a clean bowl, and sift the caster sugar and egg white powder over the egg whites. Whisk with an electric mixer until stiff peaks form.

3 In a separate bowl, sift together the icing sugar and ground almonds. Add the egg white mixture to the almond mixture. Dip a cocktail stick (toothpick) into the food colouring gel, and scrape this on to the tip of a spatula. Use the spatula to fold the mixture gently, until the colour is even and the batter falls in ribbons when lifted with the spatula.

4 Fill the piping bag with the mixture and pipe 24 4cm/1½in rounds on to the lined baking tray. Sprinkle half the shells with a few salt flakes (these will be the tops). Preheat the oven to 130°C/250°F/Gas ½, and leave the baking tray out in a warm, dry room for 15 minutes.

5 Place the tray in the middle of the oven and bake for 10 minutes. Remove from the oven and allow to cool.

6 To fill the macarons, place a teaspoonful of dulce de leche on to the flat side of an undecorated macaron shell, and top with the flat side of a decorated macaron shell. Repeat to make 12 macarons.

Per Macaron: Energy 128kcal/541kJ; Protein 2.9g; Carbohydrate 21.9g, of which sugars 21.7g; Fat 3.9g, of which saturates 0.9g; Cholesterol 4mg; Calcium 43mg; Fibre 0g; Sodium 36mg

Banoffee macarons

Sweet and indulgent, banoffee pie is one of my favourite desserts. Here, I have tried to recreate those flavours in this macaron recipe. As an alternative filling, try whipped cream drizzled with caramel.

Makes | 12 macarons

For the shells
60g/2¼oz egg whites
60g/2¼oz/generous ¼ cup caster (superfine) sugar
7.5ml/1½ tsp egg white powder
120g/4¼oz/generous 1 cup icing (confectioners') sugar
50g/2oz/½ cup ground almonds
10g/¼oz ground dried banana chips
yellow food colouring gel

For the filling
80g/3¾oz/scant ¾ cup icing (confectioners') sugar
40g/1½oz/3 tbsp unsalted butter, softened
20ml/4 tsp dulce de leche

COOK'S TIP
Grind dried banana chips using a mortar and pestle. They are available in health food stores.

1 Line a baking tray with non-stick baking parchment. Fit a piping (pastry) bag with a plain round tip.

2 Place the egg whites in a clean bowl, and sift the caster sugar and egg white powder over the egg whites. Whisk with an electric mixer until stiff peaks form.

3 In a separate bowl, sift together the icing sugar and ground almonds, then sift in the ground dried bananas. Mix the egg white mixture with the almond mixture. Dip a cocktail stick (toothpick) into the food colouring gel, and scrape this on to the tip of a spatula. Use the spatula to fold the mixture gently, until the colour is even and the batter falls in ribbons when lifted with the spatula.

4 Fill the piping bag with the mixture and pipe 24 4cm/1½in rounds on to the lined baking tray. Preheat the oven to 130°C/250°F/Gas ½, and leave the baking tray out in a warm, dry room for at least 15 minutes.

5 Place the tray in the middle of the oven and bake for 10 minutes. Remove from the oven and allow to cool.

6 To make the buttercream, place the icing sugar and butter in a bowl, and whisk until crumbly. Add the dulce de leche. Whisk until smooth.

7 To fill the macarons, place a teaspoonful of buttercream on to the flat side of one macaron shell and top with the flat side of another. Repeat to make 12 macarons.

Per Macaron: Energy 151kcal/635kJ; Protein 2g; Carbohydrate 24.7g, of which sugars 24.1g; Fat 5.5g, of which saturates 2.1g; Cholesterol 8mg; Calcium 19mg; Fibre 0g; Sodium 45mg

Hazelnut and chocolate macarons

Chocolate and hazelnut is a classic flavour combination, and the two ingredients work delightfully in these macarons. Chocolate and hazelnut spread makes a delicious, no-fuss filling here. As an alternative, use a caramel spread, or try filling the shells with dulce de leche.

Makes | 12 macarons

For the shells
60g/2¼oz egg whites
60g/2¼oz/generous ¼ cup caster (superfine) sugar
7.5ml/1½ tsp egg white powder
120g/4¼oz/generous 1 cup icing (confectioners') sugar
20g/¾oz/⅛ cup ground almonds
30g/1¼oz/¼ cup ground hazelnuts
brown food colouring gel
extra ground hazelnuts, for sprinkling

For the filling
60ml/4 tbsp chocolate and hazelnut spread

COOK'S **TIP**
When sifting the ground hazelnuts for the macaron shells, reserve the larger pieces that cannot pass through the sieve (strainer), and use them for sprinkling.

1 Line a baking tray with non-stick greaseproof baking paper. Fit a piping (pastry) bag with a plain round tip.

2 Place the egg whites in a clean bowl, and sift the caster sugar and egg white powder over the egg whites. Whisk with an electric mixer until stiff peaks form.

3 In a separate bowl, sift together the icing sugar, ground almonds and ground hazelnuts. Add the egg white mixture to the almond mixture. Dip a cocktail stick (toothpick) into the food colouring gel, and scrape this on to the tip of a spatula. Use the spatula to fold the mixture gently, until the colour is even and the batter falls in ribbons when lifted with the spatula.

4 Fill the piping bag with the mixture and pipe 24 4cm/1½in rounds onto the lined baking tray. Sprinkle half of these with chopped hazelnuts (these will be the tops). Preheat the oven to 130°C/250°F/Gas ½. Leave the baking tray out in a warm, dry room for 15 minutes.

5 Place the tray in the middle of the oven and bake for 10 minutes. Remove from the oven and allow to cool.

6 To fill the macarons, place a teaspoonful of chocolate and hazelnut spread on to the flat side of an undecorated macaron shell and top with the flat side of a decorated shell. Repeat to make 12 macarons.

Per Macaron: Energy 116kcal/488kJ; Protein 2.1g; Carbohydrate 19.1g, of which sugars 18.8g; Fat 4g, of which saturates 0.7g; Cholesterol 0mg; Calcium 19mg; Fibre 0.1g; Sodium 24mg

Chocolate and cherry macarons

In a classic combination, rich chocolate meets chunky cherry jam in these delicious macarons. For a more luxurious treat, try dipping these in melted dark (bittersweet) chocolate. They make lovely dinner-party morsels to be served with dessert wine in place of a pudding.

Makes | 12 macarons

For the shells
60g/2¼oz egg whites
60g/2¼oz/generous ¼ cup caster (superfine) sugar
7.5ml/1½ tsp egg white powder
120g/4¼oz/generous 1 cup icing (confectioners') sugar
50g/2oz/½ cup ground almonds
8g/¼oz unsweetened cocoa powder
red food colouring gel

For the filling
60ml/4 tbsp cherry jam or jelly

COOK'S TIP
These macarons offer the flavour of a Black Forest gâteau. You could serve them with some whipped cream, should you want to recreate the taste of the traditional German dessert in all its glory.

1 Line a baking tray with non-stick baking parchment. Fit a piping (pastry) bag with a plain round tip.

2 Place the egg whites in a clean bowl, and sift the caster sugar and egg white powder over the egg whites. Whisk with an electric whisk until stiff peaks form.

3 In a separate bowl, sift together the icing sugar, ground almonds and cocoa powder. Add the egg white mixture to the almond mixture. Dip a cocktail stick (toothpick) into the food colouring gel, and scrape this on to the tip of a spatula. Use the spatula to fold the mixture gently, until the colour is even and the batter falls in ribbons when lifted with the spatula.

4 Fill the piping bag with the mixture, and pipe 24 4cm/1½in rounds on to the lined baking tray. Preheat the oven to 130°C/250°F/Gas ½, and leave the baking tray out in a warm, dry room for at least 15 minutes.

5 Place the tray in the middle of the oven and bake for 10 minutes. Remove from the oven and allow to cool.

6 To fill the macarons, place a teaspoonful of cherry jam on to the flat side of one macaron shell and top with the flat side of another. Repeat to make 12 macarons.

Per Macaron: Energy 111kcal/472kJ; Protein 2g; Carbohydrate 21.7g, of which sugars 21.4g; Fat 2.5g, of which saturates 0.3g; Cholesterol 0mg; Calcium 14mg; Fibre 0.1g; Sodium 31mg

Mint and dark chocolate macarons

These macarons make a sophisticated after-dinner offering to be served with coffee. The pairing of mint and dark chocolate is a much-loved combination, and the little mint leaves makes them look truly special. If you want these to be more minty, add an extra drop of mint extract to the shell and filling.

Makes | 12 macarons

For the shells
60g/2¼oz egg whites
60g/2¼oz/generous ¼ cup caster (superfine) sugar
7.5ml/1½ tsp egg white powder
120g/4¼oz/generous 1 cup icing (confectioners') sugar
60g/2¼oz/generous ½ cup ground almonds
2 drops of mint extract
mint green food colouring gel

For the filling
60ml/4 tbsp single (light) cream
2 drops of mint extract
75g/3oz dark (bittersweet) chocolate, roughly chopped

For the decoration
liquid glucose
12 fresh mint leaves

COOK'S **TIP**
Add the mint leaves just before serving to keep them looking fresh and green.

1 Line a baking tray with non-stick baking parchment. Fit a piping (pastry) bag with a plain round tip.

2 Place the egg whites in a clean bowl, and sift the caster sugar and egg white powder over the egg whites. Whisk with an electric mixer until stiff peaks form.

3 In a separate bowl, sift together the icing sugar and ground almonds. Add the egg white mixture to the almond mixture. Add the mint extract. Dip a cocktail stick (toothpick) into the food colouring gel, and scrape this on to the tip of a spatula. Use the spatula to fold the mixture gently, until the colour is even and the batter falls in ribbons when lifted with the spatula.

4 Fill the piping bag with the mixture and pipe 24 4cm/1½in rounds on to the lined baking tray. Preheat the oven to 130°C/250°F/Gas ½, and leave the baking tray out in a warm, dry room for at least 15 minutes.

5 Place the tray in the middle of the oven and bake for 10 minutes. Remove from the oven and allow to cool.

6 For the filling, heat the cream in a non-stick pan over a low heat until it just starts to bubble. Add the mint extract to this and pour over the chopped chocolate while stirring constantly. Allow to cool, stirring occasionally, until thickened.

7 When you are ready to serve, dab a small amount of liquid glucose on to one side of the mint leaves and press gently on top of 12 shells, to create the tops. Place a teaspoonful of chocolate mint ganache on to the flat side of an undecorated macaron shell, and top with the flat side of a decorated shell. Repeat to make 12 macarons.

Per Macaron: Energy 135kcal/568kJ; Protein 2.5g; Carbohydrate 20.2g, of which sugars 19.9g; Fat 5.5g, of which saturates 1.9g; Cholesterol 3mg; Calcium 20mg; Fibre 0.2g; Sodium 23mg

Mocha macarons

This recipe embraces all things Italian, with a good dose of coffee, a dash of chocolate and a dollop of mascarpone. These macarons are the perfect pick-me-up for a lazy afternoon. For an impressive finish, half-dip the finished macarons in melted chocolate, and allow to cool and harden on a wire rack before serving.

Makes | 12 macarons

For the shells
60g/2¼oz egg whites
60g/2¼oz/generous ¼ cup caster (superfine) sugar
7.5ml/1½ tsp egg white powder
120g/4¼oz/generous 1 cup icing (confectioners') sugar
50g/2oz/½ cup ground almonds
5ml/1 tsp instant coffee granules
8g/¼oz unsweetened cocoa powder

For the filling
100g/3¾oz/scant ½ cup mascarpone
unsweetened cocoa powder,
  for dusting

VARIATION
For an alternative filling, try chocolate spread or a dark (bittersweet) chocolate ganache.

1 Line a baking tray with non-stick baking parchment. Fit a piping (pastry) bag with a plain round tip.

2 Place the egg whites in a clean bowl, and sift the caster sugar and egg white powder over the egg whites. Whisk with an electric whisk until stiff peaks form.

3 In a separate bowl, sift together the icing sugar, ground almonds, coffee granules, and cocoa powder. Add the egg white mixture to the almond mixture. Using a spatula, gently fold the mixture until the batter falls in ribbons when lifted with the spatula.

4 Fill the piping bag with the mixture, and pipe 24 4cm/1½in rounds on to the lined baking tray. Preheat the oven to 130°C/250°F/Gas ½, and leave the baking tray out in a warm, dry room for at least 15 minutes.

5 Place the tray in the middle of the oven and bake for 10 minutes. Remove from the oven and allow to cool.

6 For the filling, pipe the mascarpone on to the flat side of one macaron shell, dust with cocoa powder, and top with the flat side of another macaron shell. Repeat to make 12 macarons.

Per Macaron: Energy 106kcal/445kJ; Protein 2.2g; Carbohydrate 16.3g, of which sugars 16g; Fat 4g, of which saturates 1.2g; Cholesterol 5mg; Calcium 21mg; Fibre 0g; Sodium 26mg

Espresso macarons

For a great coffee hit, try these espresso macarons topped with chocolate-coated coffee beans and filled with a chocolatey coffee cream. Perfect to add an extra caffeine kick to your mid-morning coffee break, they look very elegant, each decorated with a single chocolate-coated coffee bean.

Makes | 12 macarons

For the shells
60g/2¼oz egg whites
60g/2¼oz/generous ¼ cup caster (superfine) sugar
7.5ml/1½ tsp egg white powder
120g/4¼oz/generous 1 cup icing (confectioners') sugar
60g/2¼oz/generous ½ cup ground almonds
5ml/1 tsp instant coffee granules
dark brown food colouring gel
12 chocolate-coated coffee beans

For the filling
75g/3oz dark (bittersweet) chocolate
60ml/4 tbsp single (light) cream
10ml/2 tsp instant coffee granules
black food colouring gel

COOK'S TIP
Chocolate-coated coffee beans are available from larger supermarkets.

1 Line a baking tray with non-stick baking parchment. Fit a piping (pastry) bag with a plain round tip.

2 Place the egg whites in a clean bowl, and sift the caster sugar and egg white powder over the egg whites. Whisk with an electric mixer until stiff peaks form.

3 In a separate bowl, sift together the icing sugar, ground almonds and coffee. Add the egg white mixture to the almond mixture. Dip a cocktail stick (toothpick) into the brown food colouring gel, and scrape this on to the tip of a spatula. Use the spatula to fold the mixture gently, until the colour is even and it falls in ribbons when lifted with the spatula.

4 Fill the piping bag with the mixture. Pipe 24 4cm/1½in rounds on to the baking tray. Place a chocolate-covered coffee bean on top of half the shells (these will be the tops). Preheat the oven to 130°C/250°F/Gas ½. Leave the tray out in a warm, dry room for 15 minutes.

5 Place the tray in the middle of the oven and bake for 10 minutes. Remove from the oven and allow to cool.

6 For the filling, melt the chocolate together with the cream and coffee in a non-stick pan over a low heat until well combined. Stir in a little black food colouring. Allow to cool while stirring occasionally until thickened.

7 To fill the macarons, place a teaspoonful of filling on to the flat side of an undecorated macaron shell and top with the flat side of a decorated shell. Repeat to make 12 macarons.

Per Macaron: Energy 136kcal/571kJ; Protein 2.6g; Carbohydrate 20.2g, of which sugars 19.9g; Fat 5.5g, of which saturates 1.9g; Cholesterol 3mg; Calcium 21mg; Fibre 0.2g; Sodium 24mg

Irish coffee and cream macarons

A classic Celtic combination, these macarons make the perfect mouthful of coffee, cream and whiskey. A must for all coffee lovers and a sophisticated dessert to serve at dinner parties. For an extra caffeine kick, try adding a teaspoonful of instant coffee granules to the filling before whisking. These are certainly not for children!

Makes | 12 macarons

For the shells
60g/2¼oz egg whites
60g/2¼oz/generous ¼ cup caster (superfine) sugar
7.5ml/1½ tsp egg white powder
120g/4¼oz/generous 1 cup icing (confectioners') sugar
60g/2¼oz/generous ½ cup ground almonds
5ml/1 tsp instant coffee granules

For the filling
80g/3¾oz/scant ¾ cup icing (confectioners') sugar
40g/1½oz/3 tbsp unsalted butter, softened
20ml/4 tsp Irish whiskey

COOK'S TIP
Reduce the quantity of whiskey in the filling, if the taste is too strong for your liking.

1 Line a baking tray with non-stick baking parchment. Fit a piping (pastry) bag with a plain round tip.

2 Place the egg whites in a clean bowl, and sift the caster sugar and egg white powder over the egg whites. Whisk with an electric mixer until stiff peaks form.

3 In a separate bowl, sift together the icing sugar, ground almonds and coffee. Add the egg white mixture to the almond mixture. Using a spatula, gently fold the mixture until the batter falls in ribbons when lifted with the spatula.

4 Fill the piping bag with the mixture and pipe 24 4cm/1½in rounds on to the lined baking tray. Preheat the oven to 130°C/250°F/Gas ½, and leave the baking tray out in a warm, dry room for at least 15 minutes.

5 Place the tray in the middle of the oven and bake for 10 minutes. Remove from the oven and allow to cool.

6 To make the buttercream filling, place the icing sugar and butter in a bowl, and whisk until crumbly. Add the whiskey and mix until smooth.

7 To fill the macarons, place a teaspoonful of buttercream on to the flat side of one macaron shell and top with the flat side of another macaron shell. Repeat to make 12 macarons.

Per Macaron: Energy 148kcal/624kJ; Protein 2g; Carbohydrate 23.1g, of which sugars 22.8g; Fat 5.5g, of which saturates 2g; Cholesterol 7mg; Calcium 14mg; Fibre 0g; Sodium 43mg

Vietnamese coffee and condensed milk macarons

Vietnamese coffee is usually served with condensed milk, and this combination works perfectly as a macaron flavour. The coffee does not necessarily need to be Vietnamese, so if you cannot find this in the supermarket, any dark-roasted instant coffee granules can be used instead.

Makes | 12 macarons

For the shells
60g/2¼oz egg whites
60g/2¼oz/generous ¼ cup caster (superfine) sugar
7.5ml/1½ tsp egg white powder
120g/4¼oz/generous 1 cup icing (confectioners') sugar
60g/2¼oz/generous ½ cup ground almonds
5ml/1 tsp instant Vietnamese coffee granules
brown food colouring gel

For the filling
80g/3¾oz/scant ¾ cup icing (confectioners') sugar
40g/1½oz/3 tbsp unsalted butter, softened
20ml/4 tsp condensed milk

1 Line a baking tray with non-stick baking parchment. Fit a piping (pastry) bag with a plain round tip.

2 Place the egg whites in a clean bowl, and sift the caster sugar and egg white powder over the egg whites. Whisk with an electric mixer until stiff peaks form.

3 In a separate bowl, sift together the icing sugar, ground almonds and coffee granules. Add the egg white mixture to the almond mixture. Dip a cocktail stick (toothpick) into the food colouring gel, and scrape this on to the tip of a spatula. Use the spatula to fold the mixture gently, until the colour is even and the batter falls in ribbons when lifted with the spatula.

4 Fill the piping bag with the mixture and pipe 24 4cm/1½in rounds on to the baking tray. Preheat the oven to 130°C/250°F/Gas ½, and leave the baking tray out in a warm, dry room for 15 minutes.

5 Place the tray in the middle of the oven and bake for 10 minutes. Remove from the oven and allow to cool.

6 To make the buttercream filling, place the icing sugar and butter in a bowl, and whisk until crumbly. Add the condensed milk, then whisk until smooth. To fill the macarons, place a teaspoonful of buttercream on to the flat side of one macaron shell and top with the flat side of another. Repeat to make 12 macarons.

Per Macaron: Energy 150kcal/632kJ; Protein 2.1g; Carbohydrate 24.1g, of which sugars 23.7g; Fat 5.7g, of which saturates 2.1g; Cholesterol 8mg; Calcium 19mg; Fibre 0g; Sodium 45mg

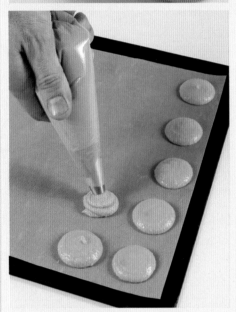

Fruity

From subtle fruity undertones to powerful
zesty kicks, the macarons in this chapter
explore the full range of flavours. Try simple
recipes made with fruit-bowl favourites,
such as apple, blueberry or apricot, or send
your tastebuds in a spin with matches made
in heaven, such as raspberry and white
chocolate, orange and quark, or coconut
and lime jelly.

Apple macarons

These macarons invoke the perfect flavour combination of apple and cinnamon. The apple buttercream gives a light and fragrant balance to the macaron shells. As an alternative, try filling the macaron shells with peeled eating apples, cut into tiny chunks and folded into some whipped cream.

Makes | 12 macarons

For the shells
60g/2¼oz egg whites
60g/2¼oz/generous ¼ cup caster (superfine) sugar
7.5ml/1½ tsp egg white powder
120g/4¼oz/generous 1 cup icing (confectioners') sugar
60g/2¼oz/generous ½ cup ground almonds
2.5ml/½ tsp ground cinnamon
pink food colouring gel

For the filling
80g/3¾oz/scant ¾ cup icing (confectioners') sugar
40g/1½oz/3 tbsp unsalted butter, softened
20ml/4 tsp apple preserve

VARIATION
Colour these macarons a pale green, if you prefer.

1 Line a baking tray with non-stick baking parchment. Fit a piping (pastry) bag with a plain round tip.

2 Place the egg whites in a clean bowl, and sift the caster sugar and egg white powder over the egg whites. Whisk with an electric mixer until stiff peaks form.

3 In a separate bowl, sift together the icing sugar, ground almonds and cinnamon. Add the egg white mixture to the almond mixture. Dip a cocktail stick (toothpick) into the colouring gel and scrape this on to the tip of a spatula. Use the spatula to fold the mixture gently, until the colour is even and the batter falls in ribbons when lifted with the spatula.

4 Fill the piping bag with the mixture and pipe 24 4cm/1½in rounds on to the lined baking tray. Preheat the oven to 130°C/250°F/Gas ½, and leave the baking tray out in a warm, dry room for at least 15 minutes.

5 Place the tray in the middle of the oven and bake for 10 minutes. Remove from the oven and allow to cool.

6 To make the buttercream filling, place the icing sugar and butter in a bowl, and whisk until crumbly. Add the apple preserve and whisk until smooth.

7 To fill the macarons, place a teaspoonful of buttercream on to the flat side of one macaron shell and top with the flat side of another macaron shell. Repeat to make 12 macarons.

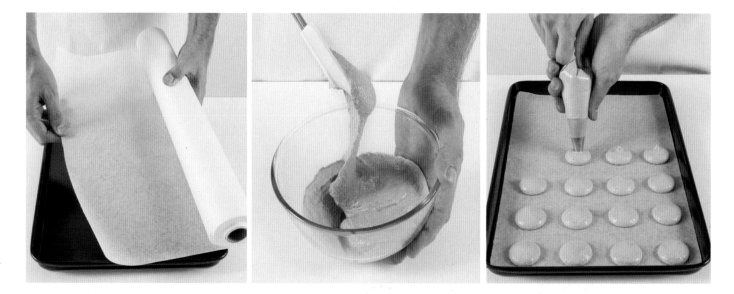

Per Macaron: Energy 146kcal/614kJ; Protein 2g; Carbohydrate 23.5g, of which sugars 23.1g; Fat 5.5g, of which saturates 2g; Cholesterol 7mg; Calcium 17mg; Fibre 0g; Sodium 43mg

Almond and pear macarons

For a light, crisp texture and fruity taste, try these almond and pear macarons. This classic flavour combination is reminiscent of a pear and almond tart. Using a teaspoon of pear preserve to fill each shell gives you an excellent balance of texture between the soft pear filling and crumbly almond shells.

Makes | 12 macarons

For the shells
60g/2¼oz egg whites
60g/2¼oz/generous ¼ cup caster (superfine) sugar
7.5ml/1½ tsp egg white powder
120g/4¼oz/generous 1 cup icing (confectioners') sugar
60g/2¼oz/generous ½ cup ground almonds
2 drops of almond extract
light green food colouring gel

For the filling
60ml/4 tbsp pear preserve

VARIATIONS
If you can obtain pear extract, add 2 drops to a basic buttercream, for an alternative filling. Whipped cream mixed with finely diced pear is also delicious.

1 Line a baking tray with non-stick baking parchment. Fit a piping (pastry) bag with a plain round tip.

2 Place the egg whites in a clean bowl, and sift the caster sugar and egg white powder over the egg whites. Whisk with an electric mixer until stiff peaks form.

3 In a separate bowl, sift together the icing sugar and ground almonds, then add the almond extract. Add the egg white mixture to the almond mixture. Dip a cocktail stick (toothpick) into the colouring gel and scrape this on to the tip of a spatula. Use the spatula to fold the mixture gently, until the colour is even and the batter falls in ribbons when lifted with the spatula.

4 Fill the piping bag with the mixture, and pipe 24 4cm/1½in rounds on to the baking tray. Preheat the oven to 130°C/250°F/Gas ½, and leave the baking tray out in a warm, dry room for 15 minutes.

5 Place the tray in the middle of the oven and bake for 10 minutes. Remove from the oven and allow to cool.

6 To fill the macarons, place a teaspoonful of pear preserve on to the flat side of one shell and top with the flat side of another. Repeat to make 12 macarons.

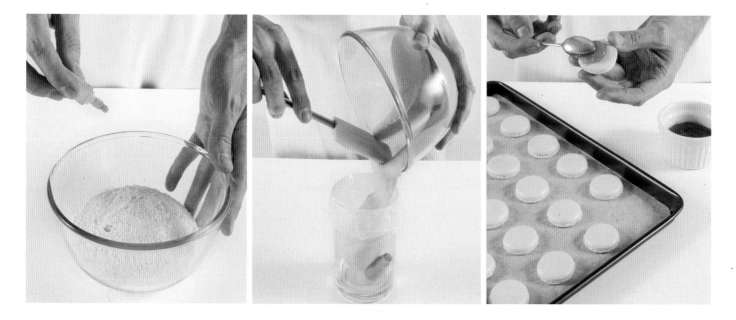

Apricot macarons

Chewy almond shells meet sweet apricot jam or jelly in these bright and colourful macarons. Another classic combination, these flavours work very well together. I sometimes like to fill these with a mixture of fresh whipped cream and chopped apricots (either fresh or dried).

Makes | 12 macarons

For the shells
60g/2¼oz egg whites
60g/2¼oz/generous ¼ cup caster (superfine) sugar
7.5ml/1½ tsp egg white powder
120g/4¼oz/generous 1 cup icing (confectioners') sugar
60g/2¼oz/generous ½ cup ground almonds
2 drops of almond extract
orange food colouring gel

For the filling
60ml/4 tbsp apricot jam or jelly

COOK'S **TIP**
Use only a tiny bit of orange food colouring at first, so that the shells do not end up too bright. You can always add more colour, but you cannot take it away!

1 Line a baking tray with non-stick greaseproof baking paper. Fit a piping (pastry) bag with a plain round tip.

2 Place the egg whites in a clean bowl, and sift the caster sugar and egg white powder over the egg whites. Whisk with an electric mixer until stiff peaks form.

3 In a separate bowl, sift together the icing sugar and ground almonds. Add the egg white mixture to the almond mixture. Add the almond extract. Dip a cocktail stick (toothpick) into the colouring gel and scrape this on to the tip of a spatula. Use the spatula to fold the mixture gently, until the colour is even and the batter falls in ribbons when lifted with the spatula.

4 Fill the piping bag with the mixture and pipe 24 4cm/1½in rounds on to the baking tray. Preheat the oven to 130°C/250°F/Gas ½, and leave the baking tray out in a warm, dry room for 15 minutes.

5 Place the tray in the middle of the oven and bake for 10 minutes. Remove from the oven and allow to cool.

6 Place a teaspoonful of apricot jam on to the flat side of one macaron shell and top with the flat side of another. Repeat to make 12 macarons.

Per Macaron: Energy 106kcal/450kJ; Protein 2g; Carbohydrate 19.6g, of which sugars 19.3g; Fat 2.8g, of which saturates 0.2g; Cholesterol 0mg; Calcium 14mg; Fibre 0g; Sodium 24mg

Cherry blossom macarons

For something truly different, try these sumptuous macarons, which evoke the taste of spring in a mouthful. Cherry blossom extract (or sakura) can be bought online. However, if you cannot obtain it, you can use natural cherry flavouring instead, or simply add some finely chopped fresh or glacé (candied) cherries to the filling.

Makes | 12 macarons

For the shells
60g/2¼oz egg whites
60g/2¼oz/generous ¼ cup caster (superfine) sugar
7.5ml/1½ tsp egg white powder
120g/4¼oz/generous 1 cup icing (confectioners') sugar
60g/2¼oz/generous ½ cup ground almonds
2 drops of cherry blossom extract
pink food colouring gel

For the filling
80g/3¾oz/scant ¾ cup icing (confectioners') sugar
40g/1½oz/3 tbsp unsalted butter, softened
20ml/4 tsp double (heavy) cream
2 drops of cherry blossom extract
pink food colouring gel

1 Line a baking tray with non-stick baking parchment. Fit a piping (pastry) bag with a plain round tip.

2 Place the egg whites in a clean bowl, and sift the caster sugar and egg white powder over the egg whites. Whisk with an electric mixer until stiff peaks form.

3 In a separate bowl, sift together the icing sugar and ground almonds. Add the egg white mixture to the almond mixture and add the cherry blossom extract. Dip a cocktail stick (toothpick) into the colouring gel and scrape this on to the tip of a spatula. Use the spatula to fold the mixture gently, until the colour is even and the batter falls in ribbons when lifted with the spatula.

4 Fill the piping bag with the mixture and pipe 24 4cm/1½in rounds on to the baking tray.

5 Preheat the oven to 130°C/250°F/ Gas ½, and leave the baking tray out in a warm, dry room for 15 minutes.

6 Place the tray in the middle of the oven and bake for 10 minutes. Remove from the oven and allow to cool.

7 To make the filling, place the icing sugar and butter in a bowl, and whisk until crumbly. Add the double cream, cherry blossom extract and a little food colouring, and continue to whisk until you have a smooth buttercream. You should aim for the shade of pink to be the same colour as the shells.

8 To fill the macarons, place a teaspoonful of buttercream on to the flat side of one macaron shell and top with the flat side of another. Repeat to make 12 macarons.

Per Macaron: Energy 153kcal/643kJ; Protein 2g; Carbohydrate 23.2g, of which sugars 22.8g; Fat 6.4g, of which saturates 2.5g; Cholesterol 9mg; Calcium 15mg; Fibre 0g; Sodium 43mg

Raspberry and white chocolate macarons

These tangy raspberry macaron shells pack a lot of flavour into a delicate mouthful. They contain freeze-dried raspberries, which have an intense flavour, and this works perfectly with the creamy white chocolate filling. This is an irresistible combination, and a firm favourite among my family and friends.

Makes | 12 macarons

For the shells
60g/2¼oz egg whites
60g/2¼oz/generous ¼ cup caster (superfine) sugar
7.5ml/1½ tsp egg white powder
120g/4¼oz/generous 1 cup icing (confectioners') sugar
50g/2oz/½ cup ground almonds
5g/⅛oz ground freeze-dried raspberries, plus extra for sprinkling

For the filling
50g/2oz white chocolate
75ml/5 tbsp double (heavy) cream

COOK'S **TIP**
Look out for breakfast cereals that contain freeze-dried raspberries – you need only a tiny amount, so you can pick out a few from there. This works out much cheaper than buying them in a packet.

1 Line a baking tray with non-stick greaseproof baking paper. Fit a piping (pastry) bag with a plain round tip.

2 Place the egg whites in a clean bowl, and sift the caster sugar and egg white powder over the egg whites. Whisk with an electric mixer until stiff peaks form.

3 In a separate bowl, sift together the icing sugar, ground almonds and freeze-dried raspberries. Add the egg white mixture to the almond mixture. Using a spatula, gently fold the mixture until the batter falls in ribbons when lifted with the spatula.

4 Fill the piping bag with the mixture, and pipe 24 4cm/1½in rounds on to the lined baking tray. Sprinkle half of the shells with the extra ground raspberries (these will be the tops). Preheat the oven to 130°C/250°F/Gas ½, and leave the baking tray out in a warm, dry room for at least 15 minutes.

5 Place the tray in the middle of the oven and bake for 10 minutes. Remove from the oven and allow to cool.

6 To make the ganache filling, melt the white chocolate with the double cream in a non-stick pan over a low heat. Remove the pan from the heat and stir occasionally, until thickened.

7 To fill the macarons, place a teaspoonful of ganache on to the flat side of an undecorated macaron shell and top with the flat side of a decorated shell. Repeat to make 12 macarons.

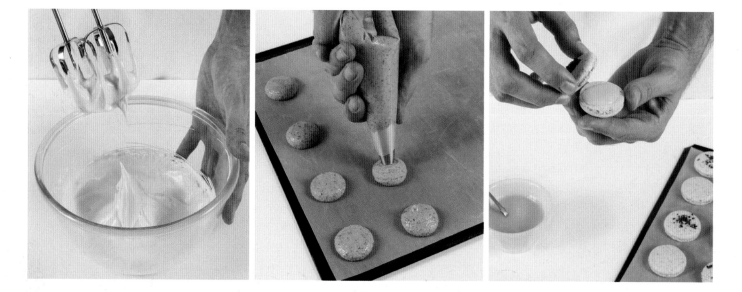

Per Macaron: Energy 141kcal/594kJ; Protein 2.3g; Carbohydrate 18.6g, of which sugars 18.4g; Fat 7g, of which saturates 3g; Cholesterol 9mg; Calcium 27mg; Fibre 0g; Sodium 27mg

Blueberry macarons

Fresh and enticing, these blueberry macarons are a stylish baby blue colour, and the filling is simply whipped cream dotted with crushed blueberries. Other berries also work well used in this way – try fresh raspberries, strawberries or blackberries, and alter the food colouring to match.

Makes | 12 macarons

For the shells
60g/2¼oz egg whites
60g/2¼oz/generous ¼ cup caster
(superfine) sugar
7.5ml/1½ tsp egg white powder
120g/4¼oz/generous 1 cup icing
(confectioners') sugar
60g/2¼oz/generous ½ cup
ground almonds
baby blue food colouring gel

For the filling
about 30 blueberries
60ml/4 tbsp whipped cream

COOK'S **TIP**
Blueberries are not as pretty inside as they are outside. Therefore, to keep the macarons as attractive as possible, do not over-crush the fruit. Stir gently into the cream.

1 Line a baking tray with non-stick baking parchment. Fit a piping (pastry) bag with a plain round tip.

2 Place the egg whites in a clean bowl, and sift the caster sugar and egg white powder over the egg whites. Whisk with an electric mixer until stiff peaks form.

3 In a separate bowl, sift together the icing sugar and ground almonds. Add the egg white mixture to the almond mixture. Dip a cocktail stick (toothpick) into the colouring gel and scrape this on to the tip of a spatula. Use the spatula to fold the mixture gently, until the colour is even and the batter falls in ribbons when lifted with the spatula.

4 Fill the piping bag with the mixture and pipe 24 4cm/1½in rounds on to the lined baking tray. Preheat the oven to 130°C/250°F/Gas ½, and leave the baking tray out in a warm, dry room for at least 15 minutes.

5 Place the tray in the middle of the oven and bake for 10 minutes. Remove from the oven and allow to cool.

6 For the filling, very lightly crush the blueberries and fold them gently into the whipped cream.

7 To fill the macarons, place a teaspoonful of the filling on to the flat side of one macaron and top with the flat side of another. Repeat to make 12 macarons.

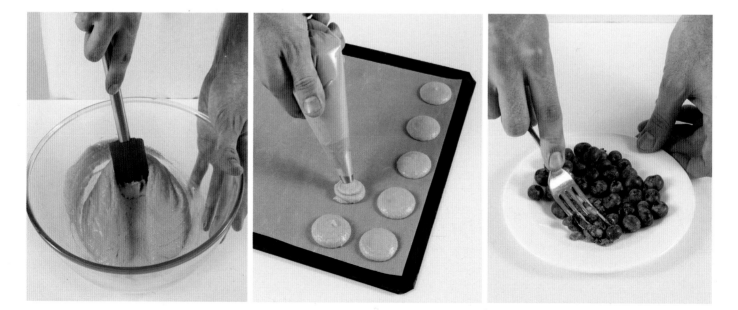

Per Macaron: Energy 114kcal/480kJ; Protein 2.1g; Carbohydrate 16.6g, of which sugars 16.3g; Fat 4.8g, of which saturates 1.5g; Cholesterol 5mg; Calcium 19mg; Fibre 0.3g; Sodium 23mg

Blackberry and lemon macarons

A sweet and tangy combination, these macarons are light with an interesting, sour kick. If freeze-dried blackberries are not readily available on their own, they can be found in some breakfast cereal packs. Such a small amount is needed, this is a clever way to obtain them!

Makes | 12 macarons

For the shells
60g/2¼oz egg whites
60g/2¼oz/generous ¼ cup caster (superfine) sugar
7.5ml/1½ tsp egg white powder
120g/4¼oz/generous 1 cup icing (confectioners') sugar
60g/2¼oz/generous ½ cup ground almonds
5g/⅛oz freeze-dried blackberries, ground
purple food colouring gel

For the filling
80g/3¾oz/scant ¾ cup icing (confectioners') sugar
40g/1½oz/3 tbsp unsalted butter, softened
20ml/4 tsp lemon curd
yellow food colouring gel

1 Line a baking tray with non-stick baking parchment. Fit a piping (pastry) bag with a plain round tip.

2 Place the egg whites in a clean bowl, and sift the caster sugar and egg white powder over the egg whites. Whisk with an electric mixer until stiff peaks form.

3 In a separate bowl, sift together the icing sugar, ground almonds and ground blackberries. Add the egg white mixture to the almond mixture. Dip a cocktail stick (toothpick) into the colouring gel and scrape this on to the tip of a spatula. Use the spatula to fold the mixture gently, until the colour is even and the batter falls in ribbons when lifted with the spatula.

4 Fill the piping bag with the mixture and pipe 24 4cm/1½in rounds on to the baking tray. Preheat the oven to 130°C/250°F/Gas ½, and leave the baking tray out in a warm, dry room for 15 minutes.

5 Place the tray in the middle of the oven and bake for 10 minutes. Remove from the oven and allow to cool.

6 To make the buttercream filling, place the icing sugar and butter in a bowl, and whisk until crumbly. Add the lemon curd and a little yellow food colouring, and whisk until smooth.

7 Place a teaspoonful of buttercream on to the flat side of one macaron shell and top with the flat side of another. Repeat to make 12 macarons.

Per Macaron: Energy 149kcal/628kJ; Protein 2g; Carbohydrate 24.2g, of which sugars 23.5g; Fat 5.6g, of which saturates 2g; Cholesterol 7mg; Calcium 14mg; Fibre 0g; Sodium 44mg

Fig macarons

Sweet and fruity, these unusual macarons capture the essence of this sumptuous fruit. Fig preserve is now widely available, and it makes a beautiful accompaniment to the crisp yet chewy macaron shells. Decorate the serving plate with some fresh figs for the ultimate figgy dessert!

Makes |12 macarons

For the shells
60g/2¼oz egg whites
60g/2¼oz/generous ¼ cup caster
  (superfine) sugar
7.5ml/1½ tsp egg white powder
120g/4¼oz/generous 1 cup icing
  (confectioners') sugar
60g/2¼oz/generous ½ cup
  ground almonds
2 drops of fig extract
purple food colouring gel

For the filling
80g/3¾oz/scant ¾ cup icing
  (confectioners') sugar
40g/1½oz/3 tbsp unsalted
  butter, softened
20ml/4 tsp fig preserve
red food colouring gel

1 Line a baking tray with non-stick baking parchment. Fit a piping (pastry) bag with a plain round tip.

2 Place the egg whites in a clean bowl, and sift the caster sugar and egg white powder over the egg whites. Whisk with an electric mixer until stiff peaks form.

3 In a separate bowl, sift together the icing sugar and ground almonds. Add the egg white mixture to the almond mixture. Add the fig extract. Dip a cocktail stick (toothpick) into the colouring gel and scrape this on to the tip of a spatula. Use the spatula to fold the mixture gently, until the colour is even and the batter falls in ribbons when lifted with the spatula.

4 Fill the piping bag with the mixture and pipe 24 4cm/1½in rounds on to the baking tray. Preheat the oven to 130°C/250°F/Gas ½, and leave the baking tray out in a warm, dry room for 15 minutes.

5 Place the tray in the middle of the oven and bake for 10 minutes. Remove from the oven and allow to cool.

6 To make the buttercream filling, place the icing sugar and butter in a bowl, and whisk until crumbly. Add the fig preserve and a little red food colouring, and whisk until smooth.

7 To fill the macarons, pipe a small amount of buttercream on to the flat side of one macaron shell and top with the flat side of another macaron shell. Repeat to make 12 macarons.

Per Macaron: Energy 149kcal/627kJ; Protein 2g; Carbohydrate 24.3g, of which sugars 24g; Fat 5.5g, of which saturates 2g; Cholesterol 7mg; Calcium 14mg; Fibre 0g; Sodium 43mg

Orange and quark macarons

Full of citrus zing, these macarons are a little cheesecake-like in their consistency and flavour combination.
You need only 1 orange for this recipe – grate the rind first for the shells, then use the juice in the filling.
I use the same colouring in the filling as the shells, which gives them an elegantly even shade all over.

Makes | 12 macarons

For the shells
60g/2¼oz egg whites
60g/2¼oz/generous ¼ cup caster
  (superfine) sugar
7.5ml/1½ tsp egg white powder
120g/4¼oz/generous 1 cup icing
  (confectioners') sugar
60g/2¼oz/generous ½ cup
  ground almonds
finely grated rind of 1 orange
orange food colouring gel

For the filling
100g/3¾oz/scant ½ cup quark
juice of 1 orange
orange food colouring gel

VARIATIONS
Instead of the fresh juice in the filling, try adding chopped orange pieces or grated orange rind.

1 Line a baking tray with non-stick baking parchment. Fit a piping (pastry) bag with a plain round tip.

2 Place the egg whites in a clean bowl, and sift the caster sugar and egg white powder over the egg whites. Whisk with an electric mixer until stiff peaks form.

3 In a separate bowl, sift together the icing sugar, ground almonds and grated orange rind. Add the egg white mixture to the almond mixture. Dip a cocktail stick (toothpick) into the colouring gel and scrape this on to the tip of a spatula. Use the spatula to fold the mixture gently, until the colour is even and the batter falls in ribbons when lifted with the spatula.

4 Fill the piping bag with the mixture and pipe 24 4cm/1½in rounds on to the baking tray. Preheat the oven to 130°C/250°F/Gas ½, and leave the baking tray out in a warm, dry room for 15 minutes.

5 Place the tray in the middle of the oven and bake for 10 minutes. Remove from the oven and allow to cool.

6 For the filling, mix the quark with the orange juice and a little food colouring.

7 Place a teaspoonful of quark mixture on to the flat side of one macaron shell and top with the flat side of another. Repeat to make 12 macarons.

Per Macaron: Energy 107kcal/451kJ; Protein 3.2g; Carbohydrate 16.8g, of which sugars 16.5g; Fat 3.5g, of which saturates 0.7g; Cholesterol 2mg; Calcium 23mg; Fibre 0g; Sodium 58mg

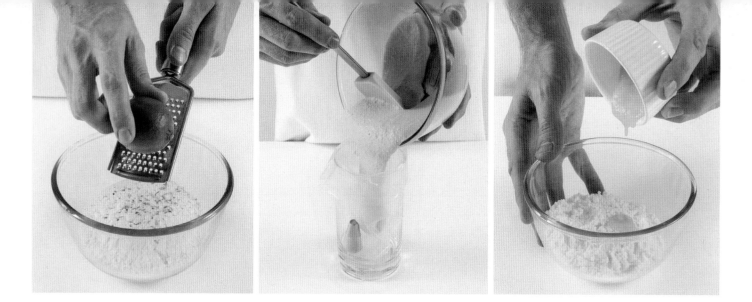

Lime and mango macarons

These macarons are totally tropical. The citrus kick of lime contrasts with the sweetness of mango in this exotic combination. These morsels are lovely on a summer's day, and are the perfect choice for a garden party or barbecue. For a refreshing change, fill the shells with lemon or lime sorbet instead, immediately before serving.

Makes | 12 macarons

For the shells
60g/2¼oz egg whites
60g/2¼oz/generous ¼ cup caster (superfine) sugar
7.5ml/1½ tsp egg white powder
120g/4¼oz/generous 1 cup icing (confectioners') sugar
60g/2¼oz/generous ½ cup ground almonds
finely grated rind of 1 lime
lime green food colouring gel

For the filling
80g/3¾oz/scant ¾ cup icing (confectioners') sugar
40g/1½oz/3 tbsp unsalted butter, softened
20ml/4 tsp mango purée (see Cook's Tip)
orange food colouring gel

COOK'S TIP
To make mango purée, process a few chunks of peeled mango in a food processor until smooth.

1 Line a baking tray with non-stick baking parchment. Fit a piping (pastry) bag with a plain round tip.

2 Place the egg whites in a clean bowl, and sift the caster sugar and egg white powder over the egg whites. Whisk with an electric mixer until stiff peaks form.

3 In a separate bowl, sift together the icing sugar and ground almonds. Add the grated lime rind. Add the egg white mixture to the almond mixture. Dip a cocktail stick (toothpick) into the colouring gel and scrape this on to the tip of a spatula. Use the spatula to fold the mixture gently, until the colour is even and the batter falls in ribbons when lifted with the spatula.

4 Fill the piping bag with the mixture and pipe 24 4cm/1½in rounds on to the baking tray. Preheat the oven to 130°C/250°F/Gas ½, and leave the baking tray out in a warm, dry room for 15 minutes.

5 Place the tray in the middle of the oven and bake for 10 minutes. Remove from the oven and allow to cool.

6 To make the buttercream filling, place the icing sugar and butter in a bowl, and whisk until crumbly. Add the mango puree and a little orange food colouring and whisk until smooth.

7 To fill the macarons, place a teaspoonful of buttercream on to the flat side of one macaron shell and top with the flat side of another. Repeat to make 12 macarons.

Per Macaron: Energy 145kcal/613kJ; Protein 2g; Carbohydrate 23.4g, of which sugars 23g; Fat 5.5g, of which saturates 2g; Cholesterol 7mg; Calcium 14mg; Fibre 0.1g; Sodium 43mg

Coconut and lime jelly macarons

For a taste of the sun, try these zingy little treats. The crisp coconut shells encase tart lime marmalade, giving a wonderful contrast of both flavour and texture. These macarons can also be filled with a spoonful of lemon or lime curd, if you prefer.

Makes | 12 macarons

For the shells
60g/2¼oz egg whites
60g/2¼oz/generous ¼ cup caster (superfine) sugar
7.5ml/1½ tsp egg white powder
120g/4¼oz/generous 1 cup icing (confectioners') sugar
40g/1½oz/⅓ cup ground almonds
20g/¾oz/⅕ cup ground desiccated (dry unsweetened shredded) coconut, plus extra for sprinkling

For the filling
60ml/4 tbsp lime marmalade

VARIATION
For a more coconutty filling, whip some coconut cream with double (heavy) cream, and add desiccated (dry unsweetened shredded) coconut and grated lime rind.

1 Line a baking tray with non-stick baking parchment. Fit a piping (pastry) bag with a plain round tip.

2 Place the egg whites in a clean bowl, and sift the caster sugar and egg white powder over the egg whites. Whisk with an electric mixer until stiff peaks form.

3 In a separate bowl, sift together the icing sugar, ground almonds and coconut. Add the egg white mixture to the almond mixture. Using a spatula, gently fold the macaron shell mixture until the batter falls in ribbons when lifted with the spatula.

4 Fill the piping bag with the mixture and pipe 24 4cm/1½in rounds on to the lined baking tray. Sprinkle half the shells liberally with desiccated coconut (these will be the tops). Preheat the oven to 130°C/250°F/Gas ½, and leave the baking tray out in a warm, dry room for at least 15 minutes.

5 Place the tray in the middle of the oven and bake for 10 minutes. Remove from the oven and allow to cool.

6 To fill the macarons, place a teaspoonful of lime marmalade on to the flat side of an undecorated macaron shell and top with the flat side of a decorated shell. Repeat to make 12 macarons.

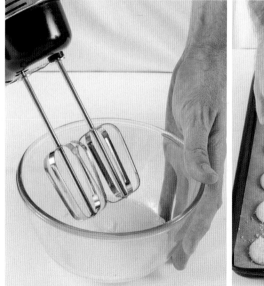

Per Macaron: Energy 101kcal/429kJ; Protein 1.8g; Carbohydrate 19.5g, of which sugars 19.3g; Fat 2.3g, of which saturates 0.2g; Cholesterol 0mg; Calcium 14mg; Fibre 0g; Sodium 25mg

Nuts, Seeds and Spices

Add some crunch to your macarons with the divine selection of recipes here. By replacing a proportion of the ground almonds with ground hazelnuts, walnuts, pecans, macadamias, cashews, pine nuts or sesame seeds, you can introduce a whole new element to your macaron shells. I have also used a variety of spices, such as cinnamon, cardamom and ginger, that really give some oomph.

Pecan and maple macarons

These macaron shells are made with ground pecans, and contain no ground almonds at all. Reminiscent of the classic American dessert, pecan pie, the crisp pecan shells are filled with rich and sweet maple butter, which oozes out deliciously. Good-quality maple syrup can be expensive, but the flavour is wonderful.

Makes | 12 macarons

For the shells
60g/2¼oz egg whites
60g/2¼oz/generous ¼ cup caster (superfine) sugar
7.5ml/1½ tsp egg white powder
120g/4¼oz/generous 1 cup icing (confectioners') sugar
60g/2¼oz/generous ½ cup ground pecans, plus extra for sprinkling

For the filling
50g/2oz/¼ cup unsalted butter, softened
50g/2oz/scant ⅙ cup maple syrup

COOK'S **TIP**
To make the macaron shell mixture more stable, substitute half the ground pecans for ground almonds.

1 Line a baking tray with non-stick baking parchment. Fit a piping (pastry) bag with a plain round tip.

2 Place the egg whites in a clean bowl, and sift the caster sugar and egg white powder over the egg whites. Whisk with an electric mixer until stiff peaks form.

3 In a separate bowl, sift together the icing sugar and ground pecans. Add the egg white mixture to the pecan mixture. Using a spatula, gently fold the mixture until the batter falls in ribbons when lifted with the spatula.

4 Fill the piping bag with the mixture and pipe 24 4cm/1½in rounds on to the lined baking tray. Sprinkle half the piped macaron shells with the extra chopped pecans (these will be the tops). Preheat the oven to 130°C/250°F/Gas ½, and leave the baking tray out in a warm, dry room for at least 15 minutes.

5 Place the tray in the middle of the oven and bake for 10 minutes. Remove from the oven and allow to cool.

6 To make the maple butter, whisk the butter in a bowl until smooth, then add the syrup and whisk well. Refrigerate until firm enough to spread.

7 To fill the macarons, spread a little maple butter on to the flat side of an undecorated macaron shell, and top with the flat side of a decorated shell. Repeat to make 12 macarons.

Per Macaron: Energy 135kcal/568kJ; Protein 2g; Carbohydrate 18.9g, of which sugars 18.4g; Fat 6.2g, of which saturates 2.4g; Cholesterol 9mg; Calcium 17mg; Fibre 0g; Sodium 47mg

Walnut macarons

Ground walnuts make a gorgeous alternative to ground almonds, and work perfectly in this recipe to form these very tasty macaron shells. Filled with a smooth walnut buttercream, and decoratively topped on one half with ground walnuts, these morsels are a nut-lover's dream.

Makes | 12 macarons

For the shells
60g/2¼oz egg whites
60g/2¼oz/generous ¼ cup caster (superfine) sugar
7.5ml/1½ tsp egg white powder
120g/4¼oz/generous 1 cup icing (confectioners') sugar
20g/¾oz/generous ⅙ cup ground almonds
40g/1½oz/generous ⅓ cup ground walnuts, plus extra for sprinkling

For the filling
80g/3¾oz/scant ¾ cup icing (confectioners') sugar
40g/1½oz/3 tbsp unsalted butter, softened
20ml/4 tsp double (heavy) cream
20ml/4 tsp ground walnuts
brown food colouring gel

1 Line a baking tray with non-stick baking parchment. Fit a piping (pastry) bag with a plain round tip.

2 Place the egg whites in a clean bowl, and sift the caster sugar and egg white powder over the egg whites. Whisk with an electric mixer until stiff peaks form.

3 In a separate bowl, sift together the icing sugar and ground walnuts. Add the egg white mixture to the walnut mixture. Gently fold the batter until it falls in ribbons when lifted with the spatula.

4 Fill the piping bag with the mixture and pipe 24 4cm/1½in rounds on to the baking tray. Carefully sprinkle ground walnuts on one side of half the shells (these will be the tops). Preheat the oven to 130°C/250°F/Gas ½, and leave the baking tray out in a warm, dry room for at least 15 minutes.

5 Place the tray in the middle of the oven and bake for 10 minutes. Remove from the oven and allow to cool.

6 To make the filling, place the icing sugar and butter in a bowl, and whisk until crumbly. Add the double cream, ground walnuts and some brown food colouring, and whisk until smooth.

7 Place a teaspoonful of buttercream on to the flat side of an undecorated shell and top with the flat side of a decorated shell. Repeat to make 12 macarons.

VARIATION
Walnut butter is a tasty alternative filling. Grind 100g/3¾oz roasted walnuts, and mix with 5ml/1 tsp clear honey and 5ml/1 tsp walnut oil, to form a thick paste.

Per Macaron: Energy 164kcal/690kJ; Protein 2.3g; Carbohydrate 23.2g, of which sugars 22.9g; Fat 7.6g, of which saturates 2.6g; Cholesterol 9mg; Calcium 16mg; Fibre 0.1g; Sodium 43mg

Chestnut macarons

Roasted chestnuts are combined beautifully with a maple butter filling in this recipe. Ready roasted and shelled chestnuts can be bought in cans to save time, or if out of season. For a special occasion, you can add a dash of champagne to the maple butter – perfect for a festive party.

Makes | 12 macarons

For the shells
60g/2¼oz egg whites
60g/2¼oz/generous ¼ cup caster (superfine) sugar
7.5ml/1½ tsp egg white powder
120g/4¼oz/generous 1 cup icing (confectioners') sugar
30g/1¼oz/generous ¼ cup ground almonds
30g/1¼oz/generous ¼ cup ground roasted chestnuts, plus extra for sprinkling (*see* Cook's Tip)

For the filling
50g/2oz/¼ cup unsalted butter, softened
50g/2oz/scant ⅙ cup maple syrup

COOK'S **TIP**
To roast chestnuts, score the top of the shells to form an X, place on to a baking tray and roast under a hot grill (broiler) or in the oven at 200°C/400°F/Gas 6, until the shells start to peel back slightly.

---

1 Line a baking tray with non-stick baking parchment. Fit a piping (pastry) bag with a plain round tip.

2 Place the egg whites in a clean bowl, and sift the caster sugar and egg white powder over the egg whites. Whisk with an electric mixer until stiff peaks form.

3 In a separate bowl, sift together the icing sugar, ground almonds and chestnuts. Add the egg white mixture to the almond mixture. Using a spatula, gently fold the mixture together until the batter falls in ribbons when lifted with the spatula.

4 Fill the piping bag with the mixture and pipe 24 4cm/1½in rounds on to the lined baking tray. Sprinkle half the piped shells with the extra ground chestnuts (these will be the tops). Preheat the oven to 130°C/250°F/Gas ½, and leave the baking tray out in a warm, dry room for at least 15 minutes.

5 Place the tray in the middle of the oven and bake for 10 minutes. Remove from the oven and allow to cool.

6 To make the maple butter filling, whisk the softened butter in a bowl until smooth, then add the syrup and whisk until combined. Refrigerate until firm enough to spread.

7 To fill the macarons, place a teaspoonful of maple butter on to the flat side of an undecorated macaron shell and top with the flat side of a decorated macaron shell. Repeat to make 12 macarons.

Per Macaron: Energy 135kcal/568kJ; Protein 2g; Carbohydrate 18.9g, of which sugars 18.4g; Fat 6.2g, of which saturates 2.4g; Cholesterol 9mg; Calcium 17mg; Fibre 0g; Sodium 47mg

Macadamia and Champagne macarons

These macarons exude elegance. The flavours are light, sophisticated and indulgent, making them a good option to serve for a special occasion. I think that they would make lovely favours at a wedding. You could sprinkle these with edible glitter for extra wow factor, if you like.

Makes | 12 macarons

For the shells
60g/2¼oz egg whites
60g/2¼oz/generous ¼ cup caster (superfine) sugar
7.5ml/1½ tsp egg white powder
120g/4¼oz/generous 1 cup icing (confectioners') sugar
30g/1¼oz/generous ¼ cup ground almonds
20g/¾oz/3½ tbsp ground macadamias, plus extra for sprinkling

For the filling
80g/3¾oz/scant ¾ cup icing (confectioners') sugar
40g/1½oz/3 tbsp unsalted butter, softened
20ml/4 tsp Champagne

1 Line a baking tray with non-stick baking parchment. Fit a piping (pastry) bag with a plain round tip.

2 Place the egg whites in a clean bowl, and sift the caster sugar and egg white powder over the egg whites. Whisk with an electric mixer until stiff peaks form.

3 In a separate bowl, sift together the icing sugar, ground almonds and macadamias. Add the egg white mixture to the almond mixture. Using a spatula, gently fold the mixture until the batter falls in ribbons when lifted with the spatula.

4 Fill the piping bag with the mixture and pipe 24 4cm/1½in rounds on to the lined baking tray. Sprinkle half the piped shells with ground macadamias (these will be the tops). Preheat the oven to 130°C/250°F/Gas ½, and leave the baking tray out in a warm, dry room for at least 15 minutes.

5 Place the tray in the middle of the oven and bake for 10 minutes. Remove from the oven and allow to cool.

6 To make the filling, place the icing sugar and butter in a bowl, and whisk until crumbly. Add the Champagne and whisk until smooth.

7 To fill the macarons, place a teaspoonful of buttercream on to the flat side of an undecorated macaron shell and top with the flat side of a decorated shell. Repeat to make 12 macarons.

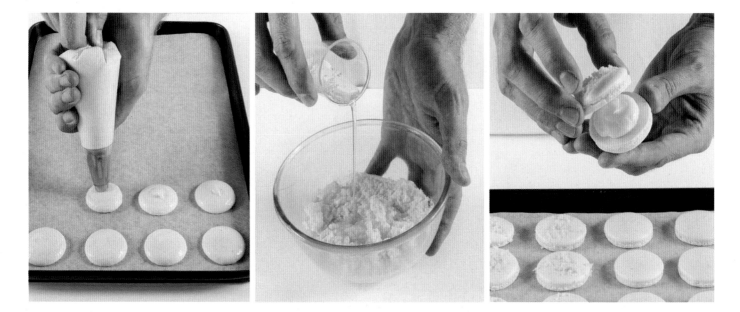

Cashew and rose macarons

These macaron shells are best made 1–2 days before serving, to allow the flavours to infuse fully. This results in a richer taste and chewier texture. If you want a more intense cashew flavour, you can toast the cashew nuts before grinding them. Make sure they are cool and finely ground before using them in the recipe.

Makes | 12 macarons

For the shells
60g/2¼oz egg whites
60g/2¼oz/generous ¼ cup caster (superfine) sugar
7.5ml/1½ tsp egg white powder
120g/4¼oz/generous 1 cup icing (confectioners') sugar
40g/1½oz/generous ⅓ cup ground cashews
20g/¾oz/3½ tbsp ground almonds
12 cashew halves, for topping

For the filling
80g/3¾oz/scant ¾ cup icing (confectioners') sugar
40g/1½oz/3 tbsp unsalted butter, softened
20ml/4 tsp double (heavy) cream
2 drops of rose extract

1 Line a baking tray with non-stick baking parchment. Fit a piping (pastry) bag with a plain round tip.

2 Place the egg whites in a clean bowl, and sift the caster sugar and egg white powder over the egg whites. Whisk with an electric mixer until stiff peaks form.

3 In a separate bowl, sift together the icing sugar, ground cashews and ground almonds. Add the egg white mixture to the cashew mixture. Gently fold the mixture together until the batter falls in ribbons when lifted with the spatula.

4 Fill the piping bag with the mixture and pipe 24 4cm/1½in rounds on to the lined baking tray. Place half a cashew on to the tops of half the macaron shells (these will be the tops). Preheat the oven to 130°C/250°F/Gas ½, and leave the baking tray out in a warm, dry room for at least 15 minutes.

5 Place the tray in the middle of the oven and bake for 10 minutes. Remove from the oven and allow to cool.

6 To make the buttercream filling, place the icing sugar and butter in a bowl, and whisk until crumbly. Add the double cream and whisk until smooth, then add the rose extract and whisk again to combine.

7 To fill the macarons, place a teaspoonful of buttercream on to the flat side of an undecorated macaron shell and top with the flat side of a decorated shell. Repeat to make 12 macarons.

Per Macaron: Energy 153kcal/643kJ; Protein 2g; Carbohydrate 23.2g, of which sugars 22.8g; Fat 6.4g, of which saturates 2.5g; Cholesterol 9mg; Calcium 15mg; Fibre 0g; Sodium 43mg

Pine nut macarons

For something a little different and exciting, this macaron flavour combination will have you 'oohing' and 'aahing' after the first bite. The savoury flavours of pine nuts and tahini combine unexpectedly with the sugar in the filling. These are very moreish – one will not be enough!

Makes | 12 macarons

For the shells
60g/2¼oz egg whites
60g/2¼oz/generous ¼ cup caster
  (superfine) sugar
7.5ml/1½ tsp egg white powder
120g/4¼oz/generous 1 cup icing
  (confectioners') sugar
60g/2¼oz/generous ½ cup ground
  pine nuts, plus extra for sprinkling

For the filling
80g/3¾oz/scant ¾ cup icing
  (confectioners') sugar
40g/1½oz/3 tbsp unsalted
  butter, softened
20ml/4 tsp tahini
10ml/2 tsp double (heavy) cream

COOK'S **TIP**
Buy a packet of whole pine nuts and grind only the amount you need.

1 Line a baking tray with non-stick baking parchment. Fit a piping (pastry) bag with a plain round tip.

2 Place the egg whites in a clean bowl, and sift the caster sugar and egg white powder over the egg whites. Whisk with an electric mixer until stiff peaks form.

3 In a separate bowl, sift together the icing sugar and ground pine nuts. Add the egg white mixture to the pine nut mixture. Using a spatula, gently fold the mixture until the batter falls in ribbons when lifted with the spatula.

4 Fill the piping bag with the mixture and pipe 24 4cm/1½in rounds on to the lined baking tray. Arrange 3 pine nuts on each of half the piped macaron shells (these will be the tops). Preheat the oven to 130°C/250°F/Gas ½, and leave the baking tray out in a warm, dry room for at least 15 minutes.

5 Place the tray in the middle of the oven and bake for 10 minutes. Remove from the oven and allow to cool.

6 To make the buttercream filling, place the icing sugar and butter in a bowl, and whisk until crumbly. Add the tahini and double cream. Whisk until smooth.

7 To fill the macarons, place a teaspoonful of buttercream on to the flat side of an undecorated macaron shell and top with the flat side of a decorated shell. Repeat to make 12 macarons.

Per Macaron: Energy 159kcal/667kJ; Protein 2.3g; Carbohydrate 23.2g, of which sugars 22.8g; Fat 7g, of which saturates 2.4g; Cholesterol 8mg; Calcium 26mg; Fibre 0.2g; Sodium 43mg

Sesame macarons

Savoury and sweet come together in these unusual macarons. You can toast the sesame seeds in a frying pan before sprinkling them over the macaron shells, for extra flavour, if you like.

Makes | 12 macarons

For the shells
60g/2¼oz egg whites
60g/2¼oz/generous ¼ cup caster (superfine) sugar
7.5ml/1½ tsp egg white powder
120g/4¼oz/generous 1 cup icing (confectioners') sugar
60g/2¼oz/generous ½ cup ground almonds
sesame seeds, for sprinkling

For the filling
80g/3¾oz/scant ¾ cup icing (confectioners') sugar
40g/1½ oz/3 tbsp unsalted butter, softened
10ml/2 tsp tahini

VARIATION
For a crunchy filling, whisk 10ml/ 2 tsp sesame seeds with 60ml/ 4 tbsp of double (heavy) cream.

1 Line a baking tray with non-stick baking parchment. Fit a piping (pastry) bag with a plain round tip.

2 Place the egg whites in a clean bowl, and sift the caster sugar and egg white powder over the egg whites. Whisk with an electric mixer until stiff peaks form.

3 In a separate bowl, sift together the icing sugar and ground almonds. Add the egg white mixture to the almond mixture. Gently fold the mixture until it falls in ribbons when lifted with the spatula.

4 Fill the piping bag with the mixture and pipe 24 4cm/1½in rounds on to the lined baking tray. Sprinkle half the shells with sesame seeds (these will be the tops). Preheat the oven to 130°C/250°F/ Gas ½. Leave the baking tray out in a warm, dry room for at least 15 minutes.

5 Place the tray in the middle of the oven and bake for 10 minutes. Remove from the oven and allow to cool.

6 To make the buttercream filling, place the icing sugar and butter in a bowl, and whisk until crumbly. Add the tahini, and whisk until smooth.

7 To fill the macarons, place a teaspoonful of buttercream on to the flat side of an undecorated macaron shell and top with the flat side of a decorated shell. Repeat to make 12 macarons.

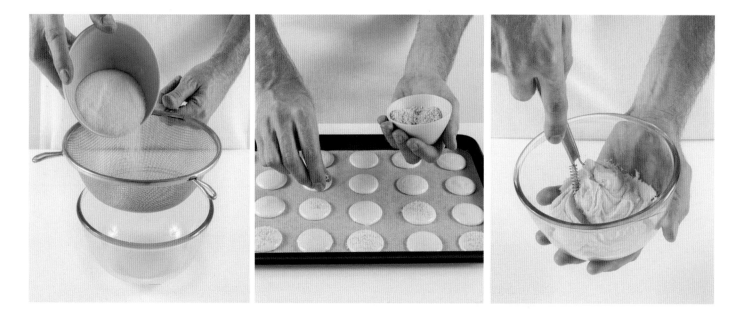

Per Macaron: Energy 149kcal/629kJ; Protein 2.1g; Carbohydrate 23.1g, of which sugars 22.8g; Fat 6g, of which saturates 2g; Cholesterol 7mg; Calcium 20mg; Fibre 0.1g; Sodium 43mg

Cinnamon macarons

These bitesize morsels provide a mouthful of winter warmth, with their comforting spice. They will evoke festive feelings, as the aroma of cinnamon fills the kitchen, and make a perfect sweet canapé for a Christmas party. A small spice shaker is useful for creating pretty lines of ground cinnamon on the shells.

Makes | 12 macarons

For the shells
60g/2¼oz egg whites
60g/2¼oz/generous ¼ cup caster (superfine) sugar
7.5ml/1½ tsp egg white powder
120g/4¼oz/generous 1 cup icing (confectioners') sugar
60g/2¼oz/generous ½ cup ground almonds
2.5ml/½ tsp ground cinnamon, plus extra for sprinkling

For the filling
80g/3¾oz/scant ¾ cup icing (confectioners') sugar
40g/1½oz/3 tbsp unsalted butter, softened
20ml/4 tsp double (heavy) cream

1 Line a baking tray with non-stick baking parchment. Fit a piping (pastry) bag with a plain round tip.

2 Place the egg whites in a clean bowl, and sift the caster sugar and egg white powder over the egg whites. Whisk with an electric mixer until stiff peaks form.

3 In a separate bowl, sift together the icing sugar, ground almonds and ground cinnamon. Add the egg white mixture to the almond mixture. Using a spatula, gently fold the mixture until the batter falls in ribbons when lifted with the spatula.

4 Fill the piping bag with the mixture and pipe 24 4cm/1½in rounds on to the lined baking tray. Sprinkle half the shells with a line of ground cinnamon (these will be the tops). Preheat the oven to 130°C/250°F/Gas ½, and leave the baking tray out in a warm, dry room for at least 15 minutes.

5 Place the tray in the middle of the oven and bake for 10 minutes. Remove from the oven and allow to cool.

6 To make the buttercream filling, place the icing sugar and butter in a bowl, and whisk until crumbly. Add the double cream and whisk until smooth.

7 To fill the macarons, place a teaspoonful of buttercream on to the flat side of an undecorated macaron shell and top with the flat side of a decorated shell. Repeat to make 12 macarons.

Energy 4665kcal/19743kJ; Protein 15g; Carbohydrate 955g, of which sugars 955g; Fat 114g, of which saturates 75g; Cholesterol 330mg; Calcium 841mg; Fibre 0g; Sodium 1157mg

Cardamom and apple macarons

These macarons offer a twist on the classic apple and cinnamon combination. Apple and cardamom form a great pairing, creating a clean, light and fresh taste in these delectable morsels. If apple preserve is not readily available, apple compote can be used to fill the macarons instead.

Makes | 12 macarons

For the shells
60g/2¼oz egg whites
60g/2¼oz/generous ¼ cup caster (superfine) sugar
7.5ml/1½ tsp egg white powder
120g/4¼oz/generous 1 cup icing (confectioners') sugar
60g/2¼oz/generous ½ cup ground almonds
2.5ml/½ tsp ground cardamom
green and brown food colouring gels

For the filling
60ml/4 tbsp apple preserve or apple compote

COOK'S **TIP**
Use equal quantities of the brown and green food colouring gels. You can add more of either colour until you have achieved the right shade.

1 Line a baking tray with non-stick baking parchment. Fit a piping (pastry) bag with a plain round tip.

2 Place the egg whites in a clean bowl, and sift the caster sugar and egg white powder over the egg whites. Whisk with an electric mixer until stiff peaks form.

3 In a separate bowl, sift together the icing sugar, ground almonds and cardamom. Add the egg white mixture to the almond mixture. Dip a cocktail stick (toothpick) into the green colouring gel and scrape this on to the tip of a spatula, repeat this with the brown colouring gel. Use the spatula to fold the mixture gently until it falls in ribbons when lifted with the spatula.

4 Fill the piping bag with the mixture and pipe 24 4cm/1½in rounds on to the baking tray. Preheat the oven to 130°C/250°F/Gas ½, and leave the baking tray out in a warm, dry room for 15 minutes.

5 Place the tray in the middle of the oven and bake for 10 minutes. Remove from the oven and allow to cool.

6 To fill the macarons, place a teaspoonful of apple preserve or compote on to the flat side of one macaron shell, and cover with the flat side of another. Repeat to make 12 macarons.

Energy 4665kcal/19743kJ; Protein 15g; Carbohydrate 955g, of which sugars 955g; Fat 114g, of which saturates 75g; Cholesterol 330mg; Calcium 841mg; Fibre 0g; Sodium 1157mg

Speculoos macarons

Festive, spicy speculoos biscuits (cookies) are usually eaten around Christmas in some European countries. It is easy to find the biscuits, as well as the speculoos paste, in large supermarkets. These macarons are full of flavour – they use a mixture of cinnamon, ginger and cloves in the shells to create the distinctive taste of speculoos biscuits, and contain smooth speculoos paste as the filling.

Makes | 12 macarons

For the shells
60g/2¼oz egg whites
60g/2¼oz/generous ¼ cup caster (superfine) sugar
7.5ml/1½ tsp egg white powder
120g/4¼oz/generous 1 cup icing (confectioners') sugar
60g/2¼oz/generous ½ cup ground almonds
1.5ml/¼ tsp ground cinnamon
1.5ml/¼ tsp ground ginger
a pinch of ground cloves

For the filling
60ml/4 tbsp speculoos paste (see Cook's Tip)

COOK'S TIP
If you cannot get hold of speculoos paste, you can make your own. Crush some speculoos biscuits (cookies) until you have fine crumbs, then mix the crumbs with enough coconut oil to form a smooth, thick paste.

1 Line a baking tray with non-stick baking parchment. Fit a piping (pastry) bag with a plain round tip

2 Place the egg whites in a clean bowl, and sift the caster sugar and egg white powder over the egg whites. Whisk with an electric mixer until stiff peaks form.

3 In a separate bowl, sift together the icing sugar, ground almonds, ground cinnamon, ground ginger and ground cloves. Add the egg white mixture to the almond mixture.

4 Dip a cocktail stick (toothpick) into the colouring gel and scrape this on to the tip of a spatula. Use the spatula to fold the mixture gently until the batter falls in ribbons when lifted with the spatula.

5 Fill the piping bag with the macaron mixture and pipe 24 4cm/1½in rounds on to the lined baking tray. Preheat the oven to 130°C/250°F/Gas ½, and leave the baking tray out in a warm, dry room for at least 15 minutes.

6 Place the tray in the middle of the oven and bake for 10 minutes. Remove from the oven and allow to cool.

7 To fill the macarons, spread a teaspoonful of speculoos paste on to the flat side of one macaron shell and top with the flat side of another. Repeat with the remaining shells and filling to make 12 macarons.

Energy 4665kcal/19743kJ; Protein 15g; Carbohydrate 955g, of which sugars 955g; Fat 114g, of which saturates 75g; Cholesterol 330mg; Calcium 841mg; Fibre 0g; Sodium 1157mg

Saffron and honey macarons

A rich and indulgent spice, saffron adds its distinctive flavour to these macaron shells, which combine perfectly with the sweet honey filling. Only a very few strands of saffron are needed, as it can be quite an overpowering flavour. When using saffron strands for decorating, I place them in a small sieve (strainer), run them under cold water, then allow them to dry before using them – this reduces the intense flavour.

Makes | 12 macarons

For the shells
60g/2¼oz egg whites
60g/2¼oz/generous ¼ cup caster (superfine) sugar
7.5ml/1½ tsp egg white powder
120g/4¼oz/generous 1 cup icing (confectioners') sugar
60g/2¼oz/generous ½ cup ground almonds
orange food colouring gel
24 saffron strands, to decorate

For the filling
80g/3¾oz/scant ¾ cup icing (confectioners') sugar
40g/1½oz/3 tbsp unsalted butter, softened
10ml/2 tsp double (heavy) cream
15ml/1 tbsp clear honey
orange food colouring gel

1 Line a baking tray with non-stick baking parchment. Fit a piping (pastry) bag with a plain round tip.

2 Place the egg whites in a clean bowl, and sift the caster sugar and egg white powder over the egg whites. Whisk with an electric mixer until stiff peaks form.

3 In a separate bowl, sift together the icing sugar, ground almonds. Add the egg white mixture to the almond mixture. Dip a cocktail stick (toothpick) into the colouring gel and scrape this on to the tip of a spatula. Use the spatula to fold the mixture gently until it falls in ribbons when lifted with the spatula.

4 Fill the piping bag with the mixture. Pipe 24 4cm/1½in rounds on to the baking tray. Top half the shells with 2 strands of saffron (these will be the tops).

5 Preheat the oven to 130°C/250°F/ Gas ½, and leave the baking tray out in a warm, dry room for at least 15 minutes.

6 Place the tray in the middle of the oven and bake for 10 minutes. Remove from the oven and allow to cool.

7 To make the honey buttercream filling, place the icing sugar and butter in a bowl, and whisk until crumbly. Add the double cream and honey, and whisk until smooth. Add a little orange food colouring gel, and mix well.

8 To fill the macarons, place a teaspoonful of buttercream on to the flat side of an undecorated macaron shell and top with the flat side of a decorated shell. Repeat to make 12 macarons.

Energy 4665kcal/19743kJ; Protein 15g; Carbohydrate 955g, of which sugars 955g; Fat 114g, of which saturates 75g; Cholesterol 330mg; Calcium 841mg; Fibre 0g; Sodium 1157mg

Candied ginger and lime macarons

Sweet with a hint of spiciness, these macaron shells are perfect with a citrus filling. The lime buttercream is easy to make, and looks stunning when coloured a vivid green. If you are short of time, the shells also work well filled with lemon curd or lime marmalade, for a quick and easy option.

Makes | 12 macarons

For the shells
60g/2¼oz egg whites
60g/2¼oz/generous ¼ cup caster (superfine) sugar
7.5ml/1½ tsp egg white powder
120g/4¼oz/generous 1 cup icing (confectioners') sugar
60g/2¼oz/generous ½ cup ground almonds
1.5ml/¼ tsp ground ginger
orange food colouring gel
10g/¼oz crystallized stem ginger, cut into small cubes, to decorate

For the filling
80g/3¾oz/scant ¾ cup icing (confectioners') sugar
40g/1½oz/3 tbsp unsalted butter, softened
10ml/2 tsp lime juice
finely grated rind of ½ lime
green food colouring gel

COOK'S TIP
If the buttercream curdles, add a little extra icing (confectioners') sugar.

1 Line a baking tray with non-stick baking parchment. Fit a piping (pastry) bag with a plain round tip.

2 Place the egg whites in a clean bowl, and sift the caster sugar and egg white powder over the egg whites. Whisk with an electric mixer until stiff peaks form.

3 In a separate bowl, sift together the icing sugar, ground almonds and ginger. Add the egg white mixture to the almond mixture. Dip a cocktail stick (toothpick) into the colouring gel, and scrape this on to the tip of a spatula. Use the spatula to fold the mixture gently until it falls in ribbons when lifted with the spatula.

4 Fill the piping bag with the mixture and pipe 24 4cm/1½in rounds on to the lined baking tray. Top half of the shells with 3 pieces of crystallized stem ginger (these will be the tops). Preheat the oven to 130°C/250°F/Gas ½, and leave the baking tray out in a warm, dry room for at least 15 minutes.

5 Place the tray in the middle of the oven and bake for 10 minutes. Remove from the oven and allow to cool.

6 To make the lime buttercream filling, place the icing sugar and butter in a bowl, and whisk until crumbly. Add the lime juice, grated lime rind and a little green food colouring, and whisk until the filling is smooth.

7 To fill the macarons, place a teaspoonful of lime buttercream on to the flat side of an undecorated macaron shell and top with the flat side of a decorated macaron shell. Repeat to make 12 macarons.

Energy 4665kcal/19743kJ; Protein 15g; Carbohydrate 955g, of which sugars 955g; Fat 114g, of which saturates 75g; Cholesterol 330mg; Calcium 841mg; Fibre 0g; Sodium 1157mg

Ginger and blood orange macarons

Fresh and fiery flavours meet in these exciting macarons. The tangy and sweet citrus filling marries beautifully with the crisp ginger shells. You can use other varieties of orange, instead of blood oranges, if you prefer.

Makes | 12 macarons

For the shells
60g/2¼oz egg whites
60g/2¼oz/generous ¼ cup caster (superfine) sugar
7.5ml/1½ tsp egg white powder
120g/4¼oz/generous 1 cup icing (confectioners') sugar
60g/2¼oz/generous ½ cup ground almonds
2.5ml/½ tsp ground ginger
2.5ml/½ tsp finely grated blood orange rind
orange food colouring gel

For the filling
80g/3¾oz/scant ¾ cup icing (confectioners') sugar
40g/1½oz/3 tbsp unsalted butter, softened
20ml/4 tsp blood orange jam or jelly
2.5ml/½ tsp finely grated blood orange rind
red food colouring gel

1 Line a baking tray with non-stick baking parchment. Fit a piping (pastry) bag with a plain round tip.

2 Place the egg whites in a clean bowl, and sift the caster sugar and egg white powder over the egg whites. Whisk with an electric mixer until stiff peaks form.

3 In a separate bowl, sift together the icing sugar, ground almonds and ginger. Add the grated rind. Add the egg white mixture to the almond mixture. Dip a cocktail stick (toothpick) into the orange food colouring gel, and scrape this on to the tip of a spatula. Use the spatula to fold the mixture gently until the batter falls in ribbons when lifted with the spatula.

4 Fill the piping bag with the mixture and pipe 24 4cm/1½in rounds on to the lined baking tray. Preheat the oven to 130°C/250°F/Gas ½, and leave the baking tray out in a warm, dry room for at least 15 minutes.

5 Place the tray in the middle of the oven and bake for 10 minutes. Remove from the oven and allow to cool.

6 To make the filling, place the icing sugar and butter in a bowl. Whisk until crumbly. Add the jam, rind and a little red food colouring. Whisk until smooth.

7 To fill the shells, place a teaspoonful of buttercream on to the flat side of one macaron shell and top with the flat side of another. Repeat to make 12 macarons.

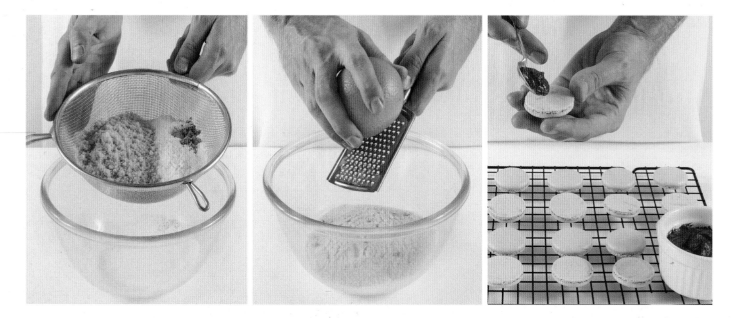

Energy 4665kcal/19743kJ; Protein 15g; Carbohydrate 955g, of which sugars 955g; Fat 114g, of which saturates 75g; Cholesterol 330mg; Calcium 841mg; Fibre 0g; Sodium 1157mg

Deliciously Different

This chapter is dedicated to the exploration of flavour combinations, with surprisingly delicious results. Try cornflakes and cream, honey and Greek yogurt, or peanut butter and jelly macarons. There are also a few recipes that bring a savoury element to these sweet bites, such as spicy wasabi and raspberry macarons, cream cheese and white pepper, and five spice and Szechuan. Go on, try them!

Honey and Greek yogurt macarons

Experience the traditional taste of Greece with these delicious macarons. The sumptuous flavour combination works effortlessly, and will instantly transport you to a sun-drenched Greek breakfast table. Use Greek honey, if you can find it, but any good-quality clear honey will work well.

Makes | 12 macarons

For the shells
60g/2¼oz egg whites
60g/2¼oz/generous ¼ cup caster (superfine) sugar
7.5ml/1½ tsp egg white powder
120g/4¼oz/generous 1 cup icing (confectioners') sugar
60g/2¼oz/generous ½ cup ground almonds
yellow food colouring gel
icing sugar, for dusting

For the filling
60ml/4 tbsp Greek (US strained plain) yogurt
15ml/1 tbsp clear honey

VARIATION
Try sprinkling half the shells with pollen grains (available from most health stores) before baking them.

1 Line a baking tray with non-stick baking parchment. Fit a piping (pastry) bag with a plain round tip.

2 Place the egg whites in a clean bowl, and sift the caster sugar and egg white powder over the egg whites. Whisk with an electric mixer until stiff peaks form.

3 In a separate bowl, sift together the icing sugar and ground almonds. Add the egg white mixture to the almond mixture. Dip a cocktail stick (toothpick) into the food colouring gel and scrape this on to the tip of a spatula. Use the spatula to fold the mixture gently until the batter falls in ribbons when lifted with the spatula.

4 Fill the piping bag with the mixture and pipe 24 4cm/1½in rounds on to the lined baking tray. Preheat the oven to 130°C/250°F/Gas ½, and leave the baking tray out in a warm, dry room for at least 15 minutes.

5 Place the tray in the middle of the oven and bake for 10 minutes. Remove from the oven and allow to cool. Dust half of the macarons with icing sugar.

6 To make the filling, mix the yogurt with the honey. Place a teaspoonful of the filling on to the flat side of a plain shell and top with the flat side of a decorated shell. Repeat to make 12 macarons.

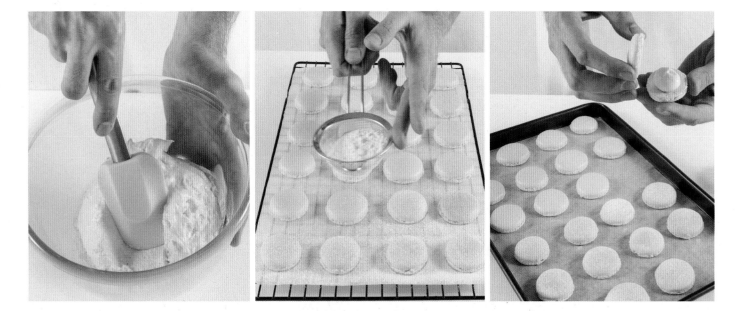

Per Macaron: Energy 102kcal/429kJ; Protein 2.2g; Carbohydrate 17.3g, of which sugars 17.1g; Fat 3.1g, of which saturates 0.4g; Cholesterol 1mg; Calcium 21mg; Fibre 0g; Sodium 29mg

Toasted bread macarons

The flavour of toast is irresistible. It is comforting and moreish, and is used to wonderful effect in these unusual macarons. If you like your toast smothered in jam or jelly, why not try spreading butter on the bottom macaron shell and jam on the top shell, then sandwiching them together?

Makes | 12 macarons

For the shells
60g/2¼oz egg whites
60g/2¼oz/generous ¼ cup caster (superfine) sugar
7.5ml/1½ tsp egg white powder
120g/4¼oz/generous 1 cup icing (confectioners') sugar
45g/1¾oz/⅔ cup ground almonds
15g/½oz/¼ cup toast crumbs (*see* Cook's Tip), plus extra for sprinkling

For the filling
80g/3¾oz/scant ¾ cup icing (confectioners') sugar
40g/1½oz/3 tbsp unsalted butter, softened
20ml/4 tsp double (heavy) cream

COOK'S TIP
You will need to scrape both sides of about 6 slices of toast.

1 Line a baking tray with non-stick baking parchment. Fit a piping (pastry) bag with a plain round tip.

2 Place the egg whites in a clean bowl, and sift the caster sugar and egg white powder over the egg whites. Whisk with an electric mixer until stiff peaks form.

3 In a separate bowl, sift together the icing sugar, ground almonds and scraped toast crumbs. Add the egg white mixture to the almond mixture. Using a spatula, gently fold the mixture until the batter falls in ribbons when lifted with the spatula.

4 Fill the piping bag with the mixture and pipe 24 4cm/1½in rounds on to the lined baking tray. Sprinkle half the piped macaron shells with the extra toast crumbs (these will be the tops). Preheat the oven to 130°C/250°F/Gas ½, and leave the baking tray out in a warm, dry room for at least 15 minutes.

5 Place the tray in the middle of the oven and bake for 10 minutes. Remove from the oven and allow to cool.

6 To make the filling, place the icing sugar and butter in a bowl, and whisk until crumbly. Add the double cream and whisk until smooth.

7 To fill the macarons, place a teaspoonful of buttercream on to the flat side of a plain macaron shell and top with the flat side of a decorated shell. Repeat to make 12 macarons.

Per Macaron: Energy 151kcal/634kJ; Protein 2g; Carbohydrate 23.7g, of which sugars 22.8g; Fat 6g, of which saturates 2.5g; Cholesterol 9mg; Calcium 15mg; Fibre 0g; Sodium 49mg

Cornflakes and cream macarons

For a fresh new take on macarons, try this wonderful recipe, which tends to be much loved by children. These macarons have a surprising light and chewy texture, and are simple to make.

Makes |12 macarons

For the shells
60g/2¼oz egg whites
60g/2¼oz/generous ¼ cup caster (superfine) sugar
7.5ml/1½ tsp egg white powder
120g/4¼oz/generous 1 cup icing (confectioners') sugar
35g/1¼oz/6½ tbsp ground almonds
25g/1oz/4⅔ tbsp ground cornflakes
yellow and brown food colouring gels
12 cornflakes, to decorate

For the filling
60ml/4 tbsp whipping cream
ground cornflakes, for sprinkling

VARIATION
For a more strongly flavoured filling, soak some cornflakes in the whipping cream overnight in the refrigerator. The next day, strain it, discarding the solids, and whip the cream until thick.

1 Line a baking tray with non-stick baking parchment. Fit a piping (pastry) bag with a plain round tip.

2 Place the egg whites in a clean bowl, and sift the caster sugar and egg white powder over the egg whites. Whisk with an electric mixer until stiff peaks form.

3 In a separate bowl, sift together the icing sugar, ground almonds and cornflakes. Add the egg white mixture to the almond mixture. Dip a cocktail stick (toothpick) into the yellow colouring gel and scrape this on to the tip of a spatula, then repeat this with the brown colouring gel. Use the spatula to fold the mixture gently until the batter falls in ribbons when lifted with the spatula.

4 Fill the piping bag with the mixture and pipe 24 4cm/1½in rounds on to the lined baking tray. Top half of these with one cornflake each (these will be the tops). Preheat the oven to 130°C/250°F/ Gas ½, and leave the baking tray out in a warm, dry room for at least 15 minutes.

5 Place the tray in the middle of the oven and bake for 10 minutes. Remove from the oven and allow to cool.

6 For the filling, whisk the cream until thick. To fill the macarons, place a teaspoonful of whipped cream on to the flat side of one undecorated macaron shell, sprinkle with ground cornflakes, and top with the flat side of a decorated shell. Repeat to make 12 macarons.

Per Macaron: Energy 111kcal/465kJ; Protein 2g; Carbohydrate 16.9g, of which sugars 16g; Fat 4.4g, of which saturates 1.5g; Cholesterol 5mg; Calcium 15mg; Fibre 0g; Sodium 31mg

Lamington macarons

The classic Australian cake has been recreated in these fabulous macarons. Every element of the traditional Lamington appears here, and they look unusual covered in chocolate and desiccated coconut.

Makes | 12 macarons

For the shells
60g/2¼oz egg whites
60g/2¼oz/generous ¼ cup caster (superfine) sugar
7.5ml/1½ tsp egg white powder
120g/4¼oz/generous 1 cup icing (confectioners') sugar
60g/2¼oz/generous ½ cup ground almonds

For the filling
60ml/4 tbsp mascarpone
30ml/2 tbsp strawberry jam (jelly)

For the covering
100g/3¾oz milk chocolate, melted
15g/½oz desiccated (dry unsweetened shredded) coconut

VARIATION
For a more elegant look, only half-dip the macarons in the chocolate.

1 Line a baking tray with non-stick baking parchment. Fit a piping (pastry) bag with a plain round tip.

2 Place the egg whites in a clean bowl, and sift the caster sugar and egg white powder over the egg whites. Whisk with an electric mixer until stiff peaks form.

3 In a separate bowl, sift together the icing sugar and ground almonds. Add the egg white mixture to the almond mixture. Using a spatula, gently fold the mixture until the batter falls in ribbons when lifted with the spatula.

4 Fill the piping bag with the mixture and pipe 24 4cm/1½in rounds on to the lined baking tray. Preheat the oven to 130°C/250°F/Gas ½, and leave the baking tray out in a warm, dry room for at least 15 minutes.

5 Place the tray in the middle of the oven and bake for 10 minutes. Remove from the oven and allow to cool.

6 To make the filling, mix the mascarpone and strawberry jam in a bowl until smooth. Place a teaspoonful of the mascarpone filling on to the flat side of one shell and top with another. Repeat to make 12 macarons.

7 Place the desiccated coconut on to a large plate or bowl, and set aside. Dip a whole macaron into the melted chocolate, and place it in the desiccated coconut (chopsticks are useful for this). Sprinkle the coconut over to coat. Place on a wire rack and allow to dry.

Per Macaron: Energy 160kcal/675kJ; Protein 2.9g; Carbohydrate 22.8g, of which sugars 22.5g; Fat 7.1g, of which saturates 3g; Cholesterol 5mg; Calcium 37mg; Fibre 0.3g; Sodium 31mg

Popcorn macarons

Fun and exciting, these macarons are excellent for a party. Both the filling and the shells include ground popcorn, which gives a bit of extra crunch. These are popular with adults and children alike, and would make a lovely surprise treat for a family movie night.

Makes | 12 macarons

For the shells
60g/2¼oz egg whites
60g/2¼oz/generous ¼ cup caster (superfine) sugar
7.5ml/1½ tsp egg white powder
120g/4¼oz/generous 1 cup icing (confectioners') sugar
50g/2oz/½ cup ground almonds
5g/⅛oz ground unsalted popcorn, plus extra to decorate

For the filling
80g/3¾oz/scant ¾ cup icing (confectioners') sugar
40g/1½oz/3 tbsp unsalted butter, softened
20ml/4 tsp double (heavy) cream
ground unsalted popcorn, for sprinkling

COOK'S TIP
Grind the popcorn in a coffee grinder or using a mortar and pestle. Any bits that do not go through the sieve (strainer) can be used for sprinkling.

1 Line a baking tray with non-stick baking parchment. Fit a piping (pastry) bag with a plain round tip.

2 Place the egg whites in a clean bowl, and sift the caster sugar and egg white powder over the egg whites. Whisk with an electric mixer until stiff peaks form.

3 In a separate bowl, sift together the icing sugar, ground almonds and ground popcorn. Add the egg white mixture to the almond mixture. Using a spatula, gently fold the mixture until the batter falls in ribbons when lifted with the spatula.

4 Fill the piping bag with the mixture and pipe 24 4cm/1½in rounds on to the lined baking tray. Sprinkle half the piped shells with the extra ground popcorn (these will be the tops). Preheat the oven to 130°C/250°F/Gas ½, and leave the baking tray out in a warm, dry room for at least 15 minutes.

5 Place the tray in the middle of the oven and bake for 10 minutes. Remove from the oven and allow to cool.

6 To make the buttercream filling, place the icing sugar and butter in a bowl, and whisk until crumbly. Add the double cream and whisk until smooth.

7 To fill the macarons, place a teaspoonful of buttercream on to the flat side of an undecorated macaron shell, sprinkle with ground popcorn, and top with the flat side of a decorated macaron shell. Repeat to make 12 macarons.

Per Macaron: Energy 150kcal/632kJ; Protein 1.9g; Carbohydrate 23.3g, of which sugars 22.8g; Fat 6.1g, of which saturates 2.5g; Cholesterol 9mg; Calcium 14mg; Fibre 0g; Sodium 43mg

Peanut butter and jelly macarons

A 'peanut butter and jelly' sandwich is a popular American snack, one that is reinvented in these innovative macarons. Grape jam or jelly is the traditional filling, but you could use another flavour, if you prefer. I used smooth peanut butter for these, but you can opt for the crunchy version, if that is more to your taste.

Makes | 12 macarons

For the shells
60g/2¼oz egg whites
60g/2¼oz/generous ¼ cup caster
(superfine) sugar
7.5ml/1½ tsp egg white powder
120g/4¼oz/generous 1 cup icing
(confectioners') sugar
60g/2¼oz/generous ½ cup
ground peanuts
12 peanut halves, for topping

For the filling
50g/2oz/¼ cup smooth peanut butter
50g/2oz/⅓ cup grape jam or jelly

COOK'S **TIP**
In the UK, 'jelly' refers to a gelatine-based dessert, so you will need grape jam or grape preserve there for this recipe. In the USA, you will need to buy grape jelly.

1 Line a baking tray with non-stick baking parchment. Fit a piping (pastry) bag with a plain round tip.

2 Place the egg whites in a clean bowl, and sift the caster sugar and egg white powder over the egg whites. Whisk with an electric mixer until stiff peaks form.

3 In a separate bowl, sift together the icing sugar and ground peanuts. Add the egg white mixture to the peanut mixture. Using a spatula, gently fold the mixture until the batter falls in ribbons when lifted with the spatula.

4 Fill the piping bag with the mixture and pipe 24 4cm/1½in rounds on to the lined baking tray. Place a peanut half on to half of the macaron shells (these will be the tops). Preheat the oven to 130°C/250°F/Gas ½, and leave the baking tray out in a warm, dry room for at least 15 minutes.

5 Place the tray in the middle of the oven and bake for 10 minutes. Remove from the oven and allow to cool.

6 To fill the macarons, place a teaspoonful of peanut butter on to the flat side of an undecorated macaron shell, and place a teaspoonful of grape jam on to the flat side of a decorated shell. Sandwich the two flat halves together. Repeat to make 12 macarons.

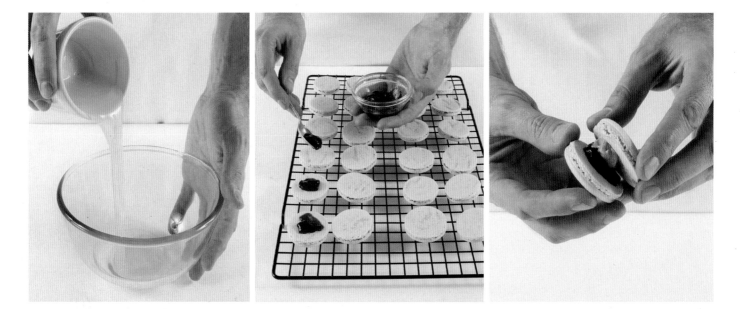

Per Macaron: Energy 130kcal/546kJ; Protein 2.9g; Carbohydrate 19.5g, of which sugars 19g; Fat 5g, of which saturates 0.8g; Cholesterol 0mg; Calcium 15mg; Fibre 0g; Sodium 38mg

Strawberry and balsamic vinegar macarons

Nothing beats the great taste of fresh strawberries in summer. When paired with a hint of balsamic vinegar, the flavour of the fruit reaches new levels of deliciousness. On a hot day, fill these shells with a spoonful of strawberry sorbet instead, and serve immediately for a truly decadent treat.

Makes | 12 macarons

For the shells
60g/2¼oz egg whites
60g/2¼oz/generous ¼ cup caster (superfine) sugar
7.5ml/1½ tsp egg white powder
120g/4¼oz/generous 1 cup icing (confectioners') sugar
50g/2oz/½ cup ground almonds
5g/⅛oz ground freeze-dried strawberries (*see* Cook's Tip, page 62)
red food colouring gel

For the filling
80g/3¾oz/scant ¾ cup icing (confectioners') sugar
40g/1½oz/3 tbsp unsalted butter, softened
10ml/2 tsp balsamic vinegar
black food colouring gel

1 Line a baking tray with non-stick baking parchment. Fit a piping (pastry) bag with a plain round tip.

2 Place the egg whites in a clean bowl, and sift the caster sugar and egg white powder over the egg whites. Whisk with an electric mixer until stiff peaks form.

3 In a separate bowl, sift together the icing sugar, ground almonds and ground strawberries. Add the egg white mixture to the almond mixture. Dip a cocktail stick (toothpick) into the red food colouring gel and scrape this on to the tip of a spatula. Use the spatula to fold the mixture gently until the batter falls in ribbons when lifted with the spatula.

4 Fill the piping bag with the mixture and pipe 24 4cm/1½in rounds on to the lined baking tray. Preheat the oven to 130°C/250°F/Gas ½, and leave the baking tray out in a warm, dry room for at least 15 minutes.

5 Place the tray in the middle of the oven and bake for 10 minutes. Remove from the oven and allow to cool.

6 To make the buttercream filling, place the icing sugar and butter in a bowl, and whisk until crumbly. Add the balsamic vinegar and a little black food colouring, and whisk until smooth.

7 To fill the shells, place a teaspoonful of buttercream on to the flat side of one shell and top with the flat side of another. Repeat to make 12 macarons.

White pepper and cream cheese macarons

Ground white pepper and cream cheese are a classic savoury combination, and they are put to excellent use in this recipe. White pepper looks elegant and lends itself surprisingly well to sweet treats, and the cheese adds some creaminess that provides a backdrop to the bolder flavours.

Makes │12 macarons

For the shells
60g/2¼oz egg whites
60g/2¼oz/generous ¼ cup caster
   (superfine) sugar
7.5ml/1½ tsp egg white powder
120g/4¼oz/generous 1 cup icing
   (confectioners') sugar
60g/2¼oz/generous ½ cup
   ground almonds
1.5ml/¼ tsp ground white pepper,
   plus extra for sprinkling

For the filling
100g/3¾oz/scant ½ cup full-fat
   cream cheese

VARIATION

I like the taste of full-fat cream cheese in these, but you can use a low-fat version for a reduced calorie count, if you prefer.

1 Line a baking tray with non-stick baking parchment. Fit a piping (pastry) bag with a plain round tip.

2 Place the egg whites in a clean bowl, and sift the caster sugar and egg white powder over the egg whites. Whisk with an electric mixer until stiff peaks form.

3 In a separate bowl, sift together the icing sugar, ground almonds and white pepper. Add the egg white mixture to the almond mixture. Using a spatula, gently fold the mixture until it falls in ribbons when lifted with the spatula.

4 Fill the piping bag with the mixture and pipe 24 4cm/1½in rounds on to the lined baking tray. Sprinkle half the shells with the extra ground white pepper (these will be the tops). Preheat the oven to 130°C/250°F/Gas ½, and leave the baking tray out in a warm, dry room for at least 15 minutes.

5 Place the tray in the middle of the oven and bake for 10 minutes. Remove from the oven and allow to cool.

6 To fill the macarons, place a teaspoonful of cream cheese on to the flat side of an undecorated macaron shell and top with the flat side of a decorated shell. Repeat to make 12 macarons.

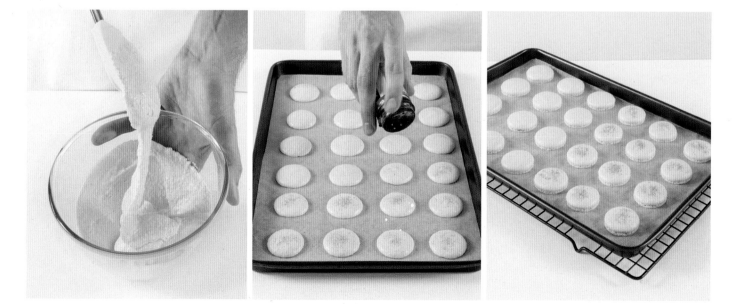

Per Macaron: Energy 130kcal/545kJ; Protein 2.2g; Carbohydrate 16.1g, of which sugars 15.9g; Fat 6.7g, of which saturates 2.7g; Cholesterol 8mg; Calcium 21mg; Fibre 0g; Sodium 46mg

Five spice and Szechuan macarons

A surprising combination, these Asian-inspired macarons bring together a mixture of warm spices and tongue-tingling Szechuan peppercorns for a very enjoyable macaron experience that will leave you wanting more.

Makes |12 macarons

For the shells
60g/2¼ oz egg whites
60g/2¼ oz/generous ¼ cup caster (superfine) sugar
7.5ml/1½ tsp egg white powder
120g/4¼ oz/generous 1 cup icing (confectioners') sugar
60g/2¼ oz/generous ½ cup ground almonds
2.5ml/½ tsp ground cinnamon
1.5ml/¼ tsp ground ginger
a small pinch ground nutmeg
a small pinch ground cloves
a small pinch ground star anise

For the filling
60ml/4 tbsp double (heavy) cream
5ml/1 tsp ground Szechuan peppercorns

1 Line a baking tray with non-stick baking parchment. Fit a piping (pastry) bag with a plain round tip.

2 Place the egg whites in a clean bowl, and sift the caster sugar and egg white powder over the egg whites. Whisk with an electric mixer until stiff peaks form.

3 In a separate bowl, sift together the icing sugar, ground almonds and spices. Add the egg white mixture to the almond mixture. Using a spatula, gently fold the mixture until it falls in ribbons when lifted with the spatula.

4 Fill the piping bag with the mixture and pipe 24 4cm/1½in rounds on to the lined baking tray. Preheat the oven to 130°C/250°F/Gas ½, and leave the baking tray out in a warm, dry room for at least 15 minutes.

5 Place the tray in the middle of the oven and bake for 10 minutes. Remove from the oven and allow to cool.

6 For the filling, whisk the double cream with the ground Szechuan peppercorns until soft folds begin to form.

7 To fill the macarons, place one teaspoonful of cream on to the flat side of one macaron shell and top with the flat side of another. Repeat to make 12 macarons.

Per Macaron: Energy 118kcal/497kJ; Protein 2.1g; Carbohydrate 16.2g, of which sugars 16g; Fat 5.5g, of which saturates 1.9g; Cholesterol 7mg; Calcium 24mg; Fibre 0g; Sodium 23mg

Wasabi and raspberry macarons

Sweet yet spicy, these macarons offer one of the most interesting flavour combinations in this book. The finished macarons are delightful in appearance, with the pretty pink filling sandwiching together pale green shells. The soft colours do belie a bit of a bite, so be sure to warn your guests!

Makes | 12 macarons

For the shells
60g/2¼oz egg whites
60g/2¼oz/generous ¼ cup caster (superfine) sugar
7.5ml/1½ tsp egg white powder
120g/4¼oz/generous 1 cup icing (confectioners') sugar
60g/2¼oz/generous ½ cup ground almonds
1.5ml/¼ tsp wasabi paste
green food colouring gel

For the filling
80g/3¾oz/scant ¾ cup icing (confectioners') sugar
40g/1½oz/3 tbsp unsalted butter, softened
20g/¾oz mashed raspberries

COOK'S TIP
Wasabi paste can be bought from Japanese stores or online.

1 Line a baking tray with non-stick baking parchment. Fit a piping (pastry) bag with a plain round tip.

2 Place the egg whites in a clean bowl, and sift the caster sugar and egg white powder over the egg whites. Whisk with an electric mixer until stiff peaks form.

3 In a separate bowl, sift together the icing sugar and ground almonds. Add the egg white mixture to the almond mixture. Scrape the wasabi paste on to the tip of a spatula. Dip a cocktail stick (toothpick) into the food colouring gel and scrape this on to the tip of the spatula. Use the spatula to fold the mixture gently until the batter falls in ribbons when lifted with the spatula.

4 Fill the piping bag with the mixture and pipe 24 4cm/1½in rounds on to the lined baking tray. Preheat the oven to 130°C/250°F/Gas ½, and leave the baking tray out in a warm, dry room for 15 minutes.

5 Place the tray in the middle of the oven and bake for 10 minutes. Remove from the oven and allow to cool.

6 To make the filling, place the icing sugar and butter in a bowl, and whisk until crumbly. Add the double cream and mashed raspberries. Whisk until smooth.

7 To fill the macarons, place a teaspoonful of buttercream on to the flat side of one macaron shell and top with the flat side of another macaron shell. Repeat to make 12 macarons.

Index

ACKNOWLEDGEMENTS

This Macarons book has been a long time coming, and I am so grateful to all those that helped me throughout! To Dondon, thank you for tasting almost all the macarons in this book and giving me feedback – your wisdom is invaluable to me. To Katiecoo, thank you for always pushing me – your friendship means the world to me. To Joanna Lorenz, thank you for allowing me to write, style and shoot this book. To Kate Eddison, thank you for all your help and wise suggestions. And last but by no means least, to Brucie, thank you very much for absolutely everything: your ideas, your food styling, your time, your patience, your support – you are my star.